My Place
A Play in Three Acts

ELAINE DUNDY

First published in 1962 by Victor Gollancz, London, 1962, copyright Elaine Dundy. The original work is in the public domain to the best of the publisher's knowledge. The publisher makes no claim to the original writings.

Names, characters, business, events, and incidents in this book are fictional. Any resemblance to actual persons, living or dead, or actual events is purely coincidental.

This edition of *My Place* is published by Giant Books, which reissues overlooked works by women writers. GiantBooks.org.

ISBN:

Print: 978-1-965751-22-0

Ebook: 978-1-965751-23-7

CHARACTERS

ANNIE FOX: A young actress, aged 25, starring in the play being presented at the theatre in which her Dressing-Room is the setting for this play.

PADDY KILMARTIN: Her boy friend. Also a young star starring in another play.

THE MOTHER: Annie's mother.

SARAH DAVENPORT: A friend of Annie's (a dressmaker). Same age as Annie.

HUW GRIFFITH MOGG: A set designer.

JOHN CROSSLEY: A Labour Candidate.

WILLY: A friend of Annie's.

HENRY RATTNER: Visitor from America.

BETTY BASSETT: Paddy's Agent.

MRS. TURNER: Annie's dresser.

A DOORMAN: New to job.

ANNIE'S UNDERSTUDY.

Action takes place in Annie's Dressing-Room

First Scene: Saturday morning round eleven o'clock

Second Scene: Saturday evening during last act of play

Third Scene: Sunday

Fourth Scene: Monday

Fifth Scene: The next Saturday

MY PLACE was first presented at the Comedy Theatre on
February 13th, 1962. The cast was as follows:

Annie Fox	DIANE CILENTO
Annie's Mother	DANDY NICHOLS
Paddy Kilmartin	BARRY FOSTER
Sarah Davenport	ANNETTE CROSBIE
Mrs. Turner	BARBARA HICKS
Assistant Stage Manager	KATE LANSBURY
An Elderly Actress	BETTY HARE
Huw Griffith Mogg	JOHN REES
An Actor	ROBERT HOLLYMAN
Willy	GUY DEGHY
John Crossley	TRISTRAM JELLINEK
Henry Rattner	HARRY TOWB
Betty Bassett	MARY JONES
Annie's Understudy	JANET MILNER

Director—JOHN Dexter

ACT I

SCENE I

Curtain goes up on a darkened room. Lighting should show that it is day time, 10 a.m. (sunlight), with the curtains drawn. There is a divan with a girl, in a slip, in bed. Door opens and woman comes in. She is dressed as for the street. Suit, hat, bag, shopping bag.

MOTHER (*coming in*): Ada? You there? What're you doing? (*Pulls one of the curtains. Lets more light in.*)

ANNIE (*sitting up*): Oh, Christ, Moma, don't do that. I'm trying to get some sleep. I was up till all hours. I'm beat.

MOTHER (*comes into room and begins to pick up clothes strewn all over. Picks up first panties, bra, very casual two-piece grey wool dress, finally black stocking-tights*): Where did you go last night?

ANNIE: To the Pigalle.

MOTHER: Ada! In these clothes! I don't know what to do about you. Here you are starring in the West End—you're earning £40 a week and you go round in these clothes and you sleep in this dressing-room.

ANNIE: O.K., O.K. Don't bug me, Moma. If that's all you've got to say why don't you split?

MOTHER: Ever since that year in America I can't make head or tail out of what you're saying. (*Thoughtfully.*) Pigalle. I think Uncle Sol's boy, Ernie, works there. Did you see him? You know, the dark-haired one? You know the one I mean? I hope you were friendly to him. I hope you weren't short. I hope you remembered to send your regards to Bernice. They've got a new baby, you know. Big blue eyes and gorgeous golden ringlets. A heart-breaker already, I'm telling you. And clever! The other day—well, you won't believe this—the other day I'm over there visiting and she comes right up to me and gives me this ball. So I roll it into a corner and what do you think she does? Lickety-split on all fours across the room, *picks it up* and brings it back to *me*! And only six months old. What do you think of that?

ANNIE: If it was a six-months-old dog you wouldn't think it so clever.

MOTHER: Well, I hope you said hello to him at least.

ANNIE: I didn't go there to see Ernie, Moma, I went to see Anita O'Day.

MOTHER: Who's that?

ANNIE: Oh God. That's what I mean. Go back to the telly. You wanted to see me, you've seen me. I'm alive. I'm well. I'm happy. Go home.

MOTHER (*lost. Drifts vaguely over to laundry bag full of dirty clothes. Takes out two slips first):* I'll just take some of these to wash out. (*She has taken out what are obviously men's pyjamas, the sight of which causes* ANNIE *to start.* MOTHER'S *reaction, however, is whether or not to wash them too. Also it starts her train of thought. Still holding on to them—*): Oh, that reminds me. I saw the most beautiful range of black lace nylon nighties in this month's *Queen.*

(ANNIE *takes pyjamas out of* MOTHER'S *hands and stuffs them under pillow in divan.* MOTHER *doesn't notice. Goes back to laundry bag.*)

And, same issue, some *very* smart chiffon cocktail frocks. They're all the rage, you know. Such lovely, soft, flowing skirts. You could get one of those. You know I'm always telling you, Ada, you dress too plain. too *severe* for your type. It makes you look so…look so…*poor*-looking.

ANNIE (*back on pillow. Eyes closed*): Let's have the fashion scoops when I can give them the undivided attention they deserve, huh, Moma? G'night.

(*Pause.* ANNIE *feigns sleep.*)

MOTHER (*collects more laundry, puts it in her shopping bag*): Well, I suppose I could go, but I'm not seeing Mrs. Miller until five o'clock. You sure you won't come and just have a cup of tea with me? Do you good.

ANNIE (*impatiently*): Split and don't try to blackmail me with the laundry bit. I can send it out. I've got the bread.

MOTHER (*sits forlornly*): Ada, can't I enjoy your success with you a little? Why won't you let me share it? After all, I did bring you up, you know. I *am* your mother.

ANNIE (*flings pillow away, sits up*): Yeah, that's right. You brought me up. That's dead right. You had a ball with me—you and the neighbours. Get her, thinks she's going to be a film star, she does. Who are we today, Ada—Rita Hayworth or Shirley Temple? Oh, it was killing. Those L.C.C. voice lessons I couldn't practise in my room during the day, your coffee klatch was so dying from laughter listening in the parlour. Every night I had to wait till you got going on that old Singer machine, so I'd be drowned out. That was fun. Look. Let's get this straight. Everything I wanted to do, everything I did, I did over your dead body. Right? Right. The scenes before I was allowed to take singing lessons, dancing lessons! God, you'd think I was studying to become a criminal. And Poppa! How is dear father? Still praying for my soul?

MOTHER: Your father is a very religious man, Ada.

ANNIE: My father is a nut. Remember how I shortened his life—what was it—ten years—by appearing in a revue in tights? Broke your own heart, too, that did. So now that I've succeeded you suddenly spring back to life, broken heart and all, and step in and say I'll take the credit, she's mine. Well I'm not yours. I'm my own creation. (*Falls back limp.*) God, I've got a hangover.

MOTHER (*rifling through her shopping bag*): Here, I brought you some of those kechels you like so much.

(*Puts parcel on divan.*)

ANNIE (*still prostrate, murmurs faintly*): My own creation. Off on my own pink cloud. (*Pulls herself up. Pats divan cover, searching round.*) Where the hell are those cigarettes?

MOTHER: I believe I've got some. (*Fumbles in her enormous handbag. Comes up with a tiny cigarette-case.*) Here, Ada, have one of mine. Go on. I'll smoke one too.

ANNIE: Ta.

(MOTHER *offers* ANNIE *cigarette with a flourish. Puts one in her own mouth. Rummages for cigarette-lighter. Tries to light* ANNIE'S. *Has trouble with lighter. She has not used it often. Lights* ANNIE'S. *Lights her own. This is near disaster. She cannot get it lit. Screws up her face and backs away from it. Looks at end of it. It is not lit. Tries again.*)

(*Despairing.*) Moma, Moma, drag in.

(MOTHER *takes a big drag and blows out smoke, coughing furiously.* ANNIE *lies back on divan again.* MOTHER *holds cigarette very elegantly with little finger crooked, the epitome of sophistication, except every time she draws on cigarette, she is covered in clouds of smoke, which she fans away elegantly with her hands.*)

MOTHER (*leaning back in the chair feeling very much in the swim*): Mrs. Shattuck's daughter saw the play the other night and complained they couldn't hear you clearly, darling, but I told her off. I said what do you expect you're such a cheap skate, you won't pay a guinea, you don't deserve to hear. Imagine the nerve!

ANNIE: Yes, Mother. And now I really do have to have a nap. I'm being interviewed at one-thirty.

MOTHER (*eagerly*): You're going on the telly again? There's a little girl on now looks just like you used to! She does a commercial for some paper napkins. She looks so cute.

ANNIE: No, it's for a magazine called *Encore*.

MOTHER: What's that?
> (ANNIE *groans*.)
> Well, darling, how am I supposed to know?

ANNIE: You're not. Can't you accept that there're things you're
    not supposed to know about me and things I'm not supposed
    to know about you? That makes us even.

MOTHER: What things?

ANNIE: Don't mix me up.

MOTHER: You coming out, Sunday?

ANNIE: If I can.

MOTHER: Your cousin Etta's going to bring her children over to
    see you. Her mother's not well. She's getting on. Could you
    get them a couple of seats for next Friday? I said you would.

ANNIE: It's only the hardest night of the week. I don't think I can
    do it.

MOTHER (*busy with laundry*): That's nice, dear. And guess
    who's seeing it tonight?

ANNIE: Don't tell me. Surprise me.

MOTHER (*roguishly*): Oh, you'll be surprised anyway.

ANNIE: Why?

MOTHER: So shall I tell you?

ANNIE: O.K. Tell me.

MOTHER: The Rattner boy.

ANNIE: No.

MOTHER: Yes.

ANNIE: NO.

MOTHER: Yes.

ANNIE: You're kidding.

MOTHER: Yes—I mean no.

ANNIE: Who the hell is the Rattner boy?

MOTHER: Why you remember, dear. His father with the big feet? Down the road where the Friedmans live now. He had the biggest feet I've ever seen. But you were crazy about him because he used to pretend he was taking a sixpence out of your ear. Fooled you every time. Of course you were only five. And the card tricks! Personally, between you and me, I think he was a bit of a card shark. I never liked it when your father went over to play cards with him. They always got into a fight. Well, he's dead now, rest his soul. Don't you remember the little Rattner girl, she wore plaits when they first moved in and then she had them cut off? And a tartan skirt? I didn't like it. I thought it was most unbecoming.

ANNIE: And what did the little Rattner boy wear?

MOTHER: I can't remember. I've forgotten what he looked like.

ANNIE: Maybe you never saw him.

MOTHER: Oh, I don't think so. I would have remembered if I hadn't, wouldn't I? No, his mother rang to tell me about him coming tonight. He's just back from America. He must be four or five years older than you by now. And very well off. *She* said. Be nice if he comes backstage. He may take you out to dinner. He's not married.

ANNIE: And he's not going to marry me.

MOTHER: Why, Ada, you don't have to marry him to have supper with him.

ANNIE: Yes I do. I have to marry him because you want me to and I'm twenty-five and all the girls on my road have fifty-five babies by now. (*Kicking again.*) Get out before I throw some-thing. Stop pestering me.

MOTHER: Well there's nothing wrong with marriage.

ANNIE: There's everything wrong with marriage.

MOTHER: And just what's wrong with it, young lady?

ANNIE: For one thing it turns people into you.

MOTHER: That will do, Ada. I don't like it when you talk to me like that. You don't talk to your friends that way, I'm sure.

ANNIE: You don't talk to me like my friends talk to me. If you talked to me like *they* talked to me I wouldn't have to talk to you like this.

MOTHER (*with perfect incomprehension, but as if she expected* ANNIE *to continue*): Yes, darling?

ANNIE: Oh, forget it.

8

MOTHER: I could go and have a look at some of the shop windows. Fortnum's always has such lovely displays, don't you think? I was a bit disappointed last week, though. The hats were all *right*, I suppose…first window just the black ones…let me see now…tulle: yes, that was the large picture hat. And a shiny black straw breton, very chic. You could've carried it off quite nicely, Ada. Pity you won't wear hats with your hair. Awful models, though. Those wooden ones with no eyes-you've seen them. And then a window with all the pink ones. Made like flowers. Pink-rose petals, pink-carnation petals, tulips, and like that. I mean it was…all right…you know, but nothing *unusual*. Know what I mean?

ANNIE: What are we going to do about that photographic memory of yours, Moma? How can we harness it?

MOTHER: Oh, do you think I'm being too critical? I did like the food display that day, I will say that. A very tasteful arrangement of artichokes, asparagus and avocados with some green and red peppers and strawberries running around the border. I wish your Uncle Bill would try to make his shop window a little smarter. He's so behind times. Of course that still leaves me with most of the afternoon.

ANNIE: Why don't you take in a matinee?

MOTHER: Nothing I really want to see. I had a look at the photos outside the one next to yours. Well I mean it was shocking. Fancy, and in the West End. I don't know what decent people think these days. They look like a lot of moral degenerates, they do.

ANNIE: Isn't that what you think about me in my play?

MOTHER: Why no dear. I mean you're supposed to be an Italian girl. You're playing a foreigner.

ANNIE: But that's the whole— No. It's too early in the morning.

MOTHER: What is?

ANNIE: Nothing.

MOTHER (*who has taken clothes out of laundry bag and puts them into her shopping bag neatly folded*): Well dear, see you Sunday then. (*Holds up blouse.*) Look here, ripped. This wants a bit of sewing.

ANNIE: O.K., O.K. But go.

MOTHER (*folding it into shopping bag, cheerful*): Ta, then, you do look a bit tired. You should lie with your feet higher than your head. Its very good for you. You become quite rested. It's called the Beauty Angle. I was reading about it in *Vogue*. Well, have a nice nap, dear. Take care.

ANNIE: Bye, bye, Morna. Take care of yourself.

(*They kiss quite affectionately. Exit* MOTHER. *As soon as* MOTHER *leaves,* ANNIE *races to the closet, opens door and* PADDY *is discovered inside in his undershorts. He reaches up to the top part where hats are kept and takes down a glass of milk, bumping his head as he does.*)

PADDY: Ow, Goddamit!

ANNIE: Sorry, darling, I didn't think it would take that long.

PADDY (*rubbing brow, etc.*): No, it was very interesting. Forty quid a week? Since when are you making that?

ANNIE: All right, so I've never dared tell her how little I really get. Oh God, oh God, who that wasn't born in an orphanage has a hope? Has success spoiled Annie Fox? No, her mother has spoiled success.

(PADDY *goes over to the screen, draws it aside. Backstage dress-ing- room table revealed. Pulls window curtains revealing room to be Annie's Dressing-Room backstage of play she is in. Looks in mirror at bump.*)

PADDY: Oh, come off it, chuck. I think your mother's gorgeous. I'd love to play her sometime. (*Imitates* MOTHER.) Fancy! And in the West End. I don't know what decent people think these days.

ANNIE (*sharply*): Don't.

PADDY: What's the matter? You spend all your time telling me how much you hate her. I must say I thought you were pretty rough on the old girl myself.

ANNIE: Leave her be.

PADDY: All right then, I'll do mine. (*Imitating accent of his mother.*) "Well son, what're you up to these days? Keeping out of dem newspapers I hope. Shocking picture of you dancing about in night clubs wid all them foreign-looking girls and drinking champagne. It's not right y'know, it's not on."

ANNIE (*in Irish*): Yiss, but suppose I was to do yer dear Old Oirish Mum?

PADDY: Yeah…I see what you mean. (*Finishes milk in one gulp. Puts glass back next to milk bottle. Goes over to divan and leans forward trying to kiss* ANNIE.)

ANNIE (*arms stiff, holds him off*): Uuh—Uuh.

PADDY (*acknowledging rebuff*): Well. What were we fighting about before she came in, like?

ANNIE: Your not showing up for dinner last night. Where were you?

PADDY (*teasing*): Ah—Ah. Now you sound like your mam.

ANNIE: Listen to me, you mick ham. I mean there was George Arnold and Leslie Acker and they wanted to talk to us about a film. Do you think I care about your sleazy sex-life?

PADDY: Then why do you call it sleazy?

ANNIE: It must be the way you keep hiding it.

PADDY: And when I'm not you say I'm flaunting it.

ANNIE: You embarrassed me in front of those film jerks. I'm not forgiving you for that. What do you think they thought of you?

PADDY: Yer what, eh? What do we care what the world thinks?

ANNIE: Honey-baby-sweetie-darling, let them call you anything but don't let them call you unreliable. I'm telling you that for your own good. First rule of the theatre.

PADDY (*loses temper, grips her by the arm*): We were neither of us born in the wings, honey-baby-sweetie-darling, and don't you forget it. Don't ever, EVER, throw hunks of tradition at me. Ever. You hear?

ANNIE (*mid-air*): Hey! You know what? You're right. That's wonderful! That's beautiful! The way I slip back into the same old mangy cliches. Belt me next time I do it. (*Leans back over other side of divan and comes up with his trousers.*) Now beat it please, darling. I've already said no, haven't I? I don't know why you took them off in the first place.

PADDY: You looked so luscious asleep there when I came by just now.

ANNIE: What was wrong with coming by last night after the show?

PADDY: Oh hell, Annie, Woh. We've got a pact about all this, haven't we? I mean we're both free to come and go as we like sort of thing.

ANNIE (*propped up on one arm and looks at him thoughtfully*): Ummmm…

PADDY: Don't throw me out, darling. I don't have anyone but you.

ANNIE: You mean you haven't any place but me. Why don't you go back to your own dressing-room down the road? You've got one too.

PADDY: I'll be having a good go at it today from the four-thirty matinee on. What do you want to do afterwards on a Saturday night?

ANNIE: Nothing with you.

PADDY: Because I didn't show up last night?

ANNIE: That's right.

PADDY: O.K. What did those two bright boys—what d'you call 'em?—Arnold and Acker—have you figured out which one is which yet? I haven't.

ANNIE: I don't think I can talk to you. As a matter of fact they think they can get a hold of that Delbert Kane script we liked so much.

PADDY: What do you mean "we"? I think it's muck.

ANNIE: It's got some beautiful things in it.

PADDY: Like a whacking big part for you, eh?

ANNIE: I'm not lis-ten-ing....

PADDY: Are you kidding? You'd listen to anyone, including the ghost of Drury Lane. I've never known anyone so easily flattered and swayed as you, girl.

ANNIE (*suddenly furious*): Get out!

PADDY: I won't!

ANNIE: You will too! (*Gets up and starts pushing him out.*)

PADDY: I won't, you know.

(*In the midst melee phone rings.* ANNIE *goes to answer it.*)

ANNIE (*in perfectly normal tone*): Yes? Who? O.K. Put her through. Hello Sarah baby, how are you? Tonight? Nothing much. Some of the kids will probably fall by afterwards. Why not come and sit with me during the second performance? I get so bored. No, of course not. Coming? Good.

See you then. (*Turns to* PADDY, *still in normal tone*.) That was Sarah. She's dropping by tonight.

PADDY: She's always dropping by. Does she fancy you?

ANNIE (*laughing*): What on earth made you say that?

PADDY: She's always dropping by.

ANNIE: Well, she's my friend. And my couturier. She's brilliant.

PADDY: No, there's something funny about her. I mean she's so detached. I don't think she fancies men.

ANNIE: Just because she doesn't flip over you?

PADDY: Don't be too sure of that, girl.

ANNIE: What the hell does that mean?

PADDY: What I said. I think she likes me all right; I don't think she fancies men. Anyroad she's got a crush on you.

ANNIE: You could be right. Gee. Kind of worrying. I'll bet it's unconscious though. (*Yawns.*) Oh yes. I was just about to throw you out. Look, I forgive you, Paddy, I really do, only do get out. I made the mistake of trying to sleep over at Jim's last night and I'm in rags.

PADDY: You slept where?

ANNIE: Relax. Jim Haggard. My agent. That brand new baby of theirs wakes up every hour until six and then it just wakes up. (*Yawns again.*) Where did you stay?

PADDY: Over at Bob Stanley's again. Always welcome.

ANNIE: This trick you taught me of sleeping out of my dressing-room is real larky, but it can be exhausting. I've already talked my doorman into leaving my pint of milk here every day—he's got a thing about me. Think I could get him to let me go the whole hog and sleep in here too instead of stumbling round at ten every morning?

PADDY: Where would be the variety then?

ANNIE: Where, indeed?

PADDY: You've got to do something to keep from going nuts during a long run.

ANNIE: That you do.

PADDY: Crikey. What time is your *Encore* man coming?

ANNIE: One-thirty, why?

PADDY: I've got to be at a building in Baker Street at one o'clock.

ANNIE: You've got to *what*?

PADDY: I've got to be at a building in Baker Street.

ANNIE: Honey-baby-sweetie-darling! Come here! (*Throws her arms round him and kisses him.*)

PADDY: Hey…what's that for?

ANNIE: That's for having to be at a building in Baker Street….

PADDY: How do you mean?

ANNIE: At one o'clock.

PADDY: What?

ANNIE: Instead of a field or a parking lot.

PADDY (*baffled*): I've got to be at my dentist's.

ANNIE (*gets up and gets the alarm clock*): At one o'clock.

PADDY (*still baffled*): Yes at one o'clock. Why?

ANNIE (*sets it for one o'clock, then turns it over to see what time it is*): You'll be there….

PADDY: Wha—?
 (*Suddenly catches on and begins to smile slowly as he settles comfortably back on the divan waiting for* ANNIE *to come towards him.*)

CURTAIN

END OF ACT ONE—*SCENE ONE*

SCENE II

Dressing-Room Party.

SARAH *and* DRESSER *discovered on stage.*

SARAH *on divan reading magazine.*

SARAH *and* ANNIE. *Time: Saturday Night.*

Time development: *First part of scene takes place in few minutes before curtain falls on a scene in the last act of the play-being-performed-on-stage which we hear over the Tannoy in the dressing-room. It is a strong emotional scene and we hear some of the dialogue loud but garbled. Sound effects of loud whispers and sobs, etc. Occasional words. Annie in Italian as the au-pair girl is being accused of sleeping with the African student. She ends up confessing to the lie, being threatened otherwise with being deported.*

ANNIE *enters dressing-room streaked with tears and panting. Smiles at* SARAH, *released.*

ANNIE (*sitting down in front of dressing-table*): Oh Sarah, that one always takes it out of me. (*Throws back head, lights cigarette and begins to wipe tears and streaked make-up off.* DRESSER *hands her bowl of ice cubes, out of which she takes one or two, running them over her face and back of neck.* DRESSER *takes the dress,* ANNIE *takes off and leaves.*)

(Business during scene of getting out of one dress and into another.)

SARAH (*putting down magazine and stretching*): It sounded wonderful. Where are we now? I've lost track.

ANNIE: Won't be long now. I've got a break for about five minutes. (*Turns the Tannoy down a little.*)
(SARAH *gets up—her feet get mixed up in sheaf of telegrams scotch-taped together that have fallen down from screen in back of divan—she tacks telegrams back up on screen.*)
Thanks, Sarah. I've been meaning to do that all evening.

SARAH: Why didn't you ask her? (*Indicating* DRESSER *off-stage.*)

ANNIE: I didn't like to—don't ask me why. (*Telephone rings.*)

Hello…. What?… Who?… Oh, Mr. Haggard. (*Impatiently.*) O.K. Put him through, put him through. (*Connection done noisily; she reacts.*) Hello, Jim. What do you suppose is going on at that switchboard? It's been full of gremlins all night…. He did? Oh no, it's too much.

(SARAH *mimes: "Shall I go?"* ANNIE *turns to* SARAH, *hand over phone.*)

No, no. Stay. It's only my agent. (*Back to phone.*) Hello, yes, I'm still here. I was just talking to someone in the room…. Oh, what? Tell me quick…. (*Lets out a whoop.*) Oh no! Hooray. So old Herbert S. Greely came through! You're sure now? Sure he can't back out… Oh, that's marvellous, Jim! Thanks for getting on to me so quickly…. O.K., Jim. 'Bye. (*Hangs up. Picks up phone again immediately. Jiggles hook nervously.*) Hello, hello. Get me Stepney 5675. (*Enunciating very clearly.*) S-T-E 5-6-7-5. Hello…. That you, Moma? Listen, I've got wonderful news. My agent just rang to tell me that the New York deal's come through…. (*Humorously.*) Jesus, Moma, don't you ever listen to anything I'm talking about? This play, of course. It's all fixed now. We're definitely going to New York in September. Think of it, I'll be a star on Broadway…. Oh hell, I don't know. We didn't discuss money. Don't worry, it'll be plenty…. Look, my agent sees to all that…. Thanks a lot…. Yeah…yeah…. I'll try to see you tomorrow, really I'll try. Got to fly now. Bye. (*Hangs up; looks dazed.*)

SARAH (*goes over to hug her*): Annie, it's marvellous, I'm so happy for you!

ANNIE: I don't know. America again. The triumphant return. I'm scared. Is that all life is—conquering fear?

SARAH: I'll make you some gorgeous new clothes. You'll knock them dead. We'll miss you, Annie. They all will but I will especially. I miss you already. I won't know what to do without you.

(DRESSER *has re-entered and hands* ANNIE *her clothes. White blouse and black skirt.* ANNIE *begins to get into them.*)

ANNIE (*looks at* SARAH, *pausing in her dressing. We see she is obviously thinking about the conversation she had about* SA-RAH *with* PADDY): Oh, come on, don't say that. You must have lots of other friends.

SARAH: I don't.

ANNIE: What's with you, Sarah? You do seem to have removed yourself a bit from the hurly burly. Why's that? I mean what's wrong? Anything particularly worrying you?

SARAH (*with a laugh*): That's just it. Nothing. Nothing worries me much. Unreality I guess. Ever since the blitz sounds stopped ringing in my ears I've been drifting along from day to day cushioned in cotton-wool. Is it real? What's real? I design clothes. The material is real but I'm not. The body is real but I'm not. Do you ever get the feeling you just don't fit in anywhere?

ANNIE: Are you Jewish?

SARAH: No, why?

ANNIE: I don't know. I always think people are. Go on about unreality, though.

SARAH: You know that Civil Disobedience thing about the

Bomb? I went and sat down along Whitehall with everyone else. I thought here's something I've got feelings about-bombs and being bombed. And if I do get carted off to jail that should be real enough-that might break the glass. Well, then they started to arrest everyone, you remember. But they didn't arrest me. And I asked the policeman who had picked me up to put me on the pavement why he wasn't putting me in the van and do you know what he said? He said, "Sorry, ma'am, we haven't any more room." He knew, you see, he knew I wasn't *people*. But I'd almost made it. I'd found my-self liking the people around me so much; almost loving them. There was nothing show-off about the stand they were taking. It was the first time I'd seen people who were...well...like it was right to be. And then I wasn't al-lowed to go with them. (*Pause*.) Frightening, isn't it?

ANNIE: No—that's O.K., but it's so impersonal. Haven't you ever been in love, for instance?

SARAH: I was married once.

ANNIE: You were?

SARAH: I expect I wasn't really. Another failure. At any rate our love or whatever it was didn't die. I just woke one day and there was this stranger sleeping next to me. I'd wanted to get married like everyone else and have children, like everyone else, but I knew that the children would turn out to be like him—dream children. It was perfectly painless. I'm ashamed to say this, but when my husband left it was three days before I realized he was gone. I mean really gone for good.

ANNIE: We've got to figure that out, Sarah. Look, why don't

you—

(*Knock on door.*)

GRIFFITH: Annie????

ANNIE: Come in, come in. Who is it?

(GRIFFITH *comes in to dressing-room table.*)

GRIFFITH: Ullo-ullo!

ANNIE (*turns to him and embraces*): Griff! Honey-baby-sweetie-darling! It's the Griffin as I live and breathe. Where have you been? I haven't seen you months.

GRIFFITH: I've been everywhere. I just came up from Newcastle. I've been down there with the new Kotchner play. (*Indicating stage.*) Where're they at?

ANNIE (*turns up Tannoy*): Ooh. Just coming up for me. You two know each other?
                    (*They shake their heads.*)
Sarah Davenport, Huw Griffith Mogg. Best bloody set designer in England.

GRIFFITH: What do you mean, England? In the world. Annie, you're a schmuck.

ANNIE: Schmuck—oh, get him.

GRIFFITH: Well, you're Jewish, aren't you?

ANNIE: Sure I am. Anything wrong with that?

GRIFFITH: As a matter of fact, yes. You killed Christ, didn't you?

ANNIE: You're damned right, I did. He deserved it. And what's more if he ever tries to show his face round here again I'll do it again.

GRIFFITH: Don't get so worked up, you'll fall off my set.

ANNIE: Your set? Oh I'll give you such a punch. I'm black and blue already from your set.

GRIFFITH: Annie, you're a schmuck.

ANNIE (*hand raised as if to strike him*): Yeah? Yeah?

GRIFFITH: Easy, girl, easy. You don't want to spoil that lambent performance.

ANNIE (*back to dressing mirror*): Listen, baby, we've been running ten months. Like the pattern is set.
(GRIFFITH *sits down. Voices heard over the Tannoy and they all settle down.*)
(*Puts finishing touches on. Sits back. Deep breath. Pause. Jumps up.*) I'm on. See you on the other side, brethren. (*Exits.*)

(SARAH *and* GRIFFITH *smile pleasantly at each other. Quietly they pick up magazines and begin to read.* DRESSER *comes in and puts out drink things, arranging glasses, ice, bottles, etc. Suddenly over Tannoy voices louder and louder, culminating in a tremendous scream.* SARAH *and* GRIFFITH *simultaneously drop the magazines and look at Tannoy, then listen intently to sounds of* ANNIE *moaning.*)

GRIFFITH (*in awed whisper*): She's a marvel, isn't she? (SARAH *nods, also lost in admiration.* ANNIE *comes back, blouse all torn, hair awry, etc.*) (*Looking up from magazine.*) You raped?

ANNIE (*sarcastically looking at her clothing, etc.*): I'm raped. And twice on Saturdays.

GRIFFITH: Good. (*Back to magazine.*)

ANNIE (*gives him a look. Glances at alarm clock*): Five more minutes to go. Nu, so what's new? (*Changes into clean blouse.*)

GRIFFITH: Haven't you heard? There's a new theatre group forming. They want me to build them a theatre. Well, first they wanted to find some old disused one and repair it and all that. I wasn't interested. I told them to scrap the whole idea of the old proscenium stage and auditorium. Start afresh. They agreed.

ANNIE: They? Who're they?

GRIFFITH: Curtis, Kotchner, Hale. That lot.

ANNIE: That lot? That lot? Oh, you're so cool, baby, you really are. What do you mean, "that lot"? Those are bloody good playwrights and directors, that lot.

GRIFFITH: Who said they weren't?

ANNIE: Oh, you make me sick. So what's it all about?

GRIFFITH: I don't know. I left them last night still arguing about the constitution. They want to break away from the log-rolling of the Royal Court and the god-bothering of the Aldwych.

ANNIE: What's that mean?

GRIFFITH: I think it means they've quarrelled with both of them.

(*Roar of applause is heard over Tannoy.*)

ANNIE (*jumping up*): That's it, thank God. Have to take the curtain call. Be with you in a minute. (*Exits.*)

GRIFFITH (*to* SARAH): Have a drink?

SARAH: Gin and tonic, please.

GRIFFITH (*to* DRESSER): It's all right, Mrs. Turner. I'll fix these.

(*He goes and makes drinks. Hands one to* SARAH *and goes back for his own, by which time* ANNIE *has come back. She takes drink out of his hand.*)

ANNIE: Thanks, baby.

GRIFFITH: That was mine, schmuck.

ANNIE: So get yourself another, schmuck. There's plenty.

(*Strains of the Queen over the Tannoy, followed by announcement in careful and precise Cockney: "Attention everyone. Attention everyone. Rehearsal at three-thirty on Monday. Rehearsal at three-thirty on Monday. Principals at three-thirty, small parts at four o'clock. Very good performance tonight. Thaaank Kew!"*)

GRIFFITH: They still rehearsing this thing?

ANNIE: It's for the understudies, you jerk. Don't you know anything about the theatre?
                    (*Knock on door.*)
Let them in, will you, Mrs. Turner.

(WILLY *enters. Forty-five and fat.*)
That was fast.

(*It is immediately apparent that her attitude towards* WILLY *is quite different from hers towards any of the others: very gentle and concerned.*)

WILLY: We were just fleeing the Queen, my dear.

ANNIE: Willy, how are you? I've been 'phoning your house all day?

WILLY: It's all right, my dear. I wasn't doing anything foolish. I'm sorry if I worried you. I was in the country visiting one of my aunts. Look, Annie, I've got a charming young man outside I want you to be especially nice to. I brought him along to the play tonight to cheer him up.

ANNIE: You thought this would cheer him up?

WILLY: Well, you know—make him forget his troubles.

ANNIE: What's the matter with him?

WILLY: Something rather serious. In fact, I'm not sure that he isn't in more serious trouble than any of us are likely to be in. He's just lost an election. A by-election, rather.

GRIFFITH: What side?

WILLY: Labour.

ANNIE: Yeah…. Like being turned down for a part.

WILLY: With this difference—every time you go up for a part it turns out to be the same one.

ANNIE: Gosh that's right. I never thought of it that way. He is in trouble. Bring him in. (*She touches him tenderly*.) You O.K., really?

WILLY: I think I'm going to be, bless you.

ANNIE (*as he leaves to get his friend*): You know Griff, don't you, and Sarah.

(*Enter* JOHN—*about thirty, well dressed.*)

WILLY (*to* JOHN): Here we are—isn't it exciting?—right in the very heart of a new wave. Annie Fox and Huw Griffith Mogg, our new revolutionary set designer, and Sarah.... Uh, Sarah, are you beat too?

SARAH: I design all her clothes.

WILLY: Well then you're beat. Or a beat sympathizer. Or a beat oriented.

ANNIE (*to Labour Candidate*): Hello—ah—?

JOHN: John Crossley.

ANNIE: John. Sit down, won't you? Have a drink. Mrs. Turner....

(MRS. TURNER *circulates. They sit down.* WILLY *on floor.*)

JOHN (*jumping up enthusiastically*): By God, that was good! I must say I bawled my bloody head off. You were simply superb, you know.

ANNIE: Thank you. It's a gas, isn't it?

WILLY: I never know whether that means good or bad.

GRIFFITH: Neither does she. She only took the first-year course in American.

ANNIE: Yes, darling. And next year your thrilling tongue.
                    (*Another knock on door.*)
Mrs. Turner?

(MRS. TURNER *goes.* HENRY RATTNER *comes in. He is tall, blond, elegantly dressed and very, very good-looking.*)

RATTNER: Miss Fox?

ANNIE: Yes?

RATTNER: I'm Henry Rattner and ach-ach-hoo! (*Sneezes.*)

ANNIE: Welcome to England !

RATTNER: Sorry, 1—ach—I achooo! (*Fit of sneezing.*) God, this is awful. I do apologize. (*Wipes his nose.*) I just wanted to say how wonderful I thought you were and thank you very much and this is a small world, but—Ach-ach-ooo! This is hopeless! I've been holding it back all night.

ANNIE: That's all right. Blow away. Have a drink.

RATTNER: No, I can feel another fit coming on. I'd better get out before. If I could ring you sometime.... (*Subsides, backing away.*)

ANNIE: Please do. Here, I'll show you to the door....

(*Gets up and goes with him. Murmurs of "thanks for coming back," etc., and final loud sneeze.* ANNIE *returns smiling and still wiping her face with cleansing tissues.*)

WILLY: Who was that?

ANNIE: That was the Rattner boy.

GRIFFITH: Who the hell is the Rattner boy?

ANNIE: The little Rattner girl wore plaits until she had them cut off. And a very unbecoming tartan skirt.

GRIFFITH: So?

ANNIE: So that's her brother. So now you know.

GRIFFITH: Annie, you're a schmuck.

JOHN: No, but this play tonight. I'm simply fascinated by it. It was about something. And I'm simply fascinated by you new young people and what's been happening to the English stage in the last four or five years. It amounts to a revolution, it does, the way you've thrown it out of the drawing-room.

WILLY (*to* JOHN): Feeling the ice-cold surf of the new wave splashing over you, John? Exhilarating, isn't it? Look at her. She's too perfect, isn't she? Black stockings and everything.

ANNIE: He's right though, Willy. We are on top now. It was a revolution.

WILLY: I've never heard such bloody nonsense talked in my whole life.

ANNIE: Why, Willy, why? Go on, tell us.

WILLY: It's not a revolution, silly goose, it's a fashion. Just as twenty years ago it was the fashion for actors and actresses to dress up to the nines trailing chinchilla and buy country seats and have the vicar in for tea. Now the only way you can tell whether an actor is out of work is if he's wearing a tie. Oh, by the way, Dame Alice was out front tonight. She thought you were just divine. What a marvellous Italian accent! she said. What a clever little artist!

ANNIE (*saying a few words in Italian, then*): I can get the Italian out all right. (*Then in Cockney.*) It's only the English I've a bit of trouble with.

WILLY: It reminded the Dame of a dear little play she did at the St. James back in '37. Only, she said, she was the governess instead of the au-pair girl and it was the son of the house instead of the African Student. But she too got raped. (*Imitating Dame Alice.*) Ra-ther fun! No, it's fashion. Twenty years from now you'll be as big a cliché with your pretty black stockings and four-letter words and regional accents…

(PADDY *enters. He carries a bunch of flowers behind his back.*)

PADDY: Ullo—ullo. Talking about me?

ANNIE: As a matter of fact he was. About us, darling.

PADDY: Let him rave. (*Kisses her.*)

ANNIE: How did your show go?

PADDY (*elaborately bored*): Packed. (*Gives her flowers.*) For you, m'dear. Picked 'em meself off the barrow.

ANNIE: Flowers on Saturday night? Are you out of your skull? What am I going to do with them? They'll all be wilted by

Monday.

PADDY (*pulling a funny face and sticking them in his sweater. Very camp*): All rightie. I'll wear them meself then. (*Everyone laughs.*) I'll have a brandy, Mrs. Turner.

WILLY (*going on as if not interrupted*): Not that I mind. As a matter of fact I couldn't be more delighted with the trend. I adore seeing coloured people and the working classes on the stage. But then I'm just a dreary old queen. (*Finishes drink and gets up and pours himself another.*)

ANNIE: We're talking about the trend, see. You know—Us. Out of the drawing-room and into real life. Only John here says it's a revolution and Willy says it's a fashion.

PADDY: What about all those strip clubs? Is that a revolution or a fashion? I went to a smashing one a couple of weeks ago.

ANNIE: Please—don't make me sick.

PADDY: Don't turn up your nose. It's a very posh place. Done up all elegant like. They've even got a restaurant.

ANNIE: Goody, so you can eat the girls.

WILLY: Oh, Annie, under those black stockings you really are a hopeless prude. I die to see one. (*To* PADDY.) Do let m know when you next go. I'll come along with my shooting stick and sketching pad and motoring veil.

JOHN (*excited*): Well, I don't agree with you, Willy. I think it's more than a fashion. They say that the theatre in this country is generally ten years behind the times, but you people completed your revolution in just five years—less than that. And the English audiences are just beginning to realize that what they're seeing on stage can have some connection with their lives.

ANNIE: Tell my mother that....

JOHN: ...that it's speaking directly to them and abo t them for the first time in ages. I see a play like the one tonight and I look at that rapt audience and I take heart. And I realize that as far as the ordinary people go politics must be about twenty years behind. The body politic is the most conserva-tive of all bodies. (*To* ANNIE.) How to break through and to get to the people? That's what I've got to find out. Because what did I lose the election on—sorry about this, I just lost an election last Thursday and I'm still smarting under the blow—

ANNIE: No, go on. What did you?

JOHN: Did I lose it on my youth, on my stan on the H-bomb, Public Schools, Capital Punishment—things like that—or did I lose it because I just couldn't get through....

ANNIE: I like you! You're great! You're beautiful! When are you going to stand again? I'll go and vote for you.

JOHN: Thank you. No need for that. Just vote in your own con-stituency.

ANNIE: Gee. You know I've never voted in my life.

JOHN: Maybe that's why we're twenty years behind.

ANNIE: Oh well, I'm in the clear then. I was too young twenty years ago. (*All groan.*) Well look...I mean how many here have ever voted? You Sarah?

SARAH: Yes.

ANNIE: Willy?

WILLY: I have.

ANNIE (*incredulously*): Griffith?

GRIFFITH: Aw, come off it. What do you think? Of course I have.

ANNIE: Well…I don't know…. You Paddy?

PADDY: Nope.

> (*He hopes to get a laugh on this but they look at him instead rather quizzically. He catches this.*)

ANNIE: Hmmm. What do you suppose we've been doing all this time?

WILLY: Playing games. (*Begins snapping fingers rhythmically.*) You know, One-two-three Garnes.

ANNIE (*picking up the beat, also snapping fingers*): One-two-three Dames.

PADDY: One-two-three Blames.

SARAH: One-two-three Names.

WILLY: One-two-three Flames.

> (*All turn to* JOHN, *snapping their fingers one-two-three.* JOHN *looks confused. Reaction from the rest.*)

JOHN: I'm sorry…I don't…

ANNIE: We're playing rhyme or associate. You know, like Freud.

> (JOHN *nods his understanding.*)

One-two-three Rob.

SARAH: One-two-three Sob.

GRIFFITH: One-two-three Job.

> (*All point to* JOHN.)

JOHN: One-two-three. (*Groans.*) Oh damn!

SARAH: Job? Damn? What's the association? I challenge.

JOHN: No, it's just I couldn't...just... Yes, I see. It's a bloody good game.

WILLY: Job's enough to make anyone stumble. Why work when you can steal?

ANNIE: Hey, did you used to steal? I must have lifted half of Woolworth's in my time.

PADDY: I stole buns from the bakery.

SARAH: I stole picture postcards. I'd forgotten about it.

WILLY: I used to pinch golf balls. I'd go over with my school pals and hide in the bunkers of the local country club and make off with the balls that landed there. Then we'd sell them back to the sporting shop in the village for 6d. each. Goodness it was exciting. I look back on it as the high point of my career. Everything else has been downhill. I must be drunk already. (*To* SARAH.) Gin? (*Gets up and takes her glass and pours himself another.*)

SARAH: What do you do now? I've always wondered.

WILLY: Nothing at the moment. You know the producer of this play? Well, I'm his ex-lover. It seems to be taking up rather a lot of my time. (*Spills her drink in handing it to her.*) Sorry.

ANNIE (*earnestly*): Willy's one of the most distinguished mycologists alive.

(*Everyone laughs.*)

WILLY: There, you see?

ANNIE: Well, dammit, that's what you are!

GRIFFITH: Yes, but what is it?

ANNIE: Mushrooms, you schmuck.

GRIFFITH: I'll give you such a clout! (*Rises.*) Let's eat. I'm starving.

ANNIE: O.K. Where'll we go?

GRIFFITH: The usual. Every other restaurant's closed by now. (*To* ANNIE.) Come on. On your way.

JOHN: I'm going to have to leave you, worse luck. I said I'd go back to the country tonight. I had no idea I was going to have such a good time. Good night all of you and thanks. (*Goes to* ANNIE.) You should be proud of yourselves. (*To* GRIFFITH *and* PADDY.) All of you. You stand for something, you know.

ANNIE (*shaking his hand*): Willy, I'm mad about our Labour

M.P.

JOHN: Only I'm not a Labour M.P.

ANNIE: You want to be a Labour M.P.? You'll be one!

JOHN: Bless you for that.

ANNIE: Fall by here anytime. Always Open House.

JOHN: I'll take you up on that if I may.

ANNIE (*as they make to go, etc.*): Get out all of you a minute, will you? I want to speak to Paddy alone. We'll catch you up.

WILLY: Well hurry up for goodness sakes. I want to have my supper and then I want to get home to my bottle.

ANNIE: O.K. O.K. O.K.

(*They exit.* ANNIE *pecks* PADDY *on the cheek. Picks up a rose. Begins dancing Flamenco around him. N.B.: During follow-ing scene* DRESSER *is picking up and tidying up. They pay no attention to her nor does she to them except occasionally as a slightly interested spectator. When the roses are thrown she makes no attempt to pick them up.*)

ANNIE: Well, me foine Oirish Boyo. (*Rose in mouth.*) Guess what?

PADDY: I don't know. What?

ANNIE (*rose still in teeth*): No. Guess.

PADDY: Oh, come on, Annie. Now, don't be coy. Come out with it.

ANNIE (*rose still in teeth. In the middle of a flamenco turn*): What's eating you?

PADDY: Do you always have to make a fool of me?

ANNIE (*rose out of mouth*): About what?

PADDY: About voting.

ANNIE (*tosses roses on divan*): If you're ashamed of not voting for God's sake go out and vote. There's always someone to vote for, alderman or something. Town crier.

PADDY: It puts me right off it does, voting. There's something too law-abiding about it.

ANNIE: I couldn't agree more. It's part of our rebellion, not voting.

PADDY: Or part of our stupidity.

ANNIE: Oh, darling, don't be sad. I've got the most wonderful news. It's happened. It's finally happened.

PADDY: You're pregnant.

ANNIE: Very funny. Oh ha-ha. It's the play. Goes to Broadway in September. With me in it. A firm offer.

PADDY: You've accepted?

ANNIE: Like a shot.

PADDY: You little bitch. (*Sits on divan.*)

ANNIE: I must say you don't seem very pleased.

PADDY: You're damn right I'm not. What about me?

ANNIE: I don't dig.

PADDY: Oh, speak English, for God's sake. You only use that daft hipster talk when you're trying to put something over on me.

ANNIE: Very well. In plain English I'm perplexed by your attitude. To put it mildly. That clear enough?

PADDY: It's *your* attitude that's a bit mucky, girl. It didn't occur to you, I suppose, that before you accepted you might have had the consideration to consult me?

ANNIE: But you already knew about it. I've been talking of this possibility for six months. That's as long as we've known each other.

PADDY (*rising, standing over her*): You astonish me. You simply amaze me, you do. A girl goes with me. Goes with me hot and heavy, mind you, for six months. And the first chance I get of a job that'll take me half-way round the world from her, I jump at, without so much as a by your leave. Now I'm not very smart but I think I'd be perplexed if she wasn't a mite put out.

ANNIE: But I didn't jump. And I'm not trying to put anything over on you. I only heard it myself during the last interval tonight. Oh hell. O.K., then, I'm asking your leave. Can I go to America?

PADDY: No, you cannot.

ANNIE: Oh really? How're you going to stop me?

PADDY: I'll think of something.

ANNIE: I already have. You're just annoyed because it's me that was asked and not you!

PADDY: Oh shut up, Annie. I could have gone over there three times since I've known you.

ANNIE: Not without breaking your contract you couldn't.

PADDY (*losing his temper and gripping her by the shoulders*): You little fool. I didn't go because I wanted to stay here with you.

ANNIE: Sure, sure. Because the offers weren't tempting enough, you mean.

PADDY (*lets go of her disgusted*): All right, believe what you want. Go to New York if you want. Go to hell. Play another year in a part you've already gone dotty playing in this long. That's progress. (*Begins to leave—final shot.*) That's selling out.

ANNIE: Wait a minute. (*Picks flowers out of vase deliberately and extends them to him.*) Here. You forgot these. I don't want them moulting all over my dressing-room.

(DRESSER *by now very much in evidence at dressing-table, tidying up and straightening out jars, etc.* PADDY *snatches flowers from* ANNIE *and hurls them to the door.* ANNIE *cringes backwards squealing dramatically.*)

ANNIE: Don't think you can hit me because you're bigger than me. I'll scream.

(*During all this,* DRESSER, *occupied with dressing-table, pays absolutely no attention to the fight. At no time does she pick up or even glance at the roses.* DRESSER—MRS. TURNER—*puts away drink things and slowly works away at dressing-table. When* PADDY *throws the flowers she is putting towel on dressing-table.* DRESSER *sits down in front of dressing-table mirror. Leans forward. Sighs. Reaches into bottom drawer of table and pulls out dinner pail. Opens it up. Opens up wax paper. It looks as if she is about to pull out something to eat. Wearily she dips into pail, emerging with make-up on her finger-tips, which she obtrusively rubs into face. Then she begins to paint her face, eyes, eyebrows, lips, with more and more of a flourish as the make-up gets wilder. Combs hair forwards over one eye. Studies her bust in mirror intently. Finally opens top button of her jacket, revealing a low decolletage of sunburst pleats. Stands up and rolls top of skirt over once, shortening it. Strikes pin-up pose in mirror. Thinks it over. Reaches into lunch pail again and pulls out horn-rimmed spectacles, puts them on. Gives last satisfied look in glass and puts lunch pail away. This is worked out concurrently with the scene that follows.*)

PADDY (*moves back into room and slumps on the divan. Plays with her rose, sulking*): I wasn't going to hit you. (*Begins to eat rose petals.*)

ANNIE (*this speech should be done facing straight out front, in the manner of Comédie-Française declamation, very quietly, very still, with self-induced tears. Beautifully modulated tone*): Do you think I'm all that keen on the idea of New York? I got bounced around there like a ping-pong ball for a year and believe me Americans aren't the most understanding race in the world. They love you when you love yourself. Once you doubt yourself and need them you are through. I can show you scars to prove it. It runs with the packsville. (*Slight movement.*) But what can I do? I'm a woman. (*Pause.*)

(*Also* DRESSER *switches on low, lovely, humming fan under the speech and switches it off at this point.*)

Look down the cast list of shows on now. See how the men's parts outnumber the women's at least three to two every time. God, your play hasn't even got one woman in it. Neither has Ross. Neither has *Beyond the Fringe*. And then, maybe I'm not all that easy to cast. My agent's looking around every day for a good property for me.

PADDY: Oh God…now we switch to expense account jargon. I think I prefer the hip stuff.

ANNIE: Yes, Property. I like the word. It sounds corrupt. Oh come on, we're all dying to see if they can corrupt us. You're no different from the rest. You're dying to be a big international star too.

PADDY: International star my eye. There's no such thing. Even Olivier isn't a big international star. Show me an international star and I'll show you a lousy actor.

ANNIE: Spencer Tracy. Cary Grant.

PADDY: How do you know they're good? Ever seen them on the stage?

ANNIE: Now you're splitting hairs. (*Looks up and sees that* DRESSER *has completed her business at dressing-table.*) That'll be all, Mrs. Turner. Have a nice week-end.

(*Neither* PADDY *nor* ANNIE *shows any surprise at her transformation.*)

PADDY (*chewing on rose petals*): 'Night, Mrs. Turner.
(DRESSER *exits.*)
Why are we talking about Spencer Tracy?

ANNIE: I don't know. America. You don't want me to go.

PADDY (*sliding down from divan on to oar, almost inaudibly*):
No.

ANNIE (*goes over to him and sits on oar beside him*): What is it,
darling? Tell me.

PADDY: I'm afraid. Don't leave me. You'll go off and leave me
and you'll never come back. You'll be swinging in New
York with all that hip crowd. Whatever that means. Whatever anything means. God, what an ignorant bastard I am! I
can spend a whole evening with some of these West End
characters and not understand a word they're saying.

ANNIE: Like the film people you didn't show up for the other
night?

PADDY: What a bunch of comic bleeders that lot is! Capital gains
and percentages and losses. They sound like a bunch of
bloody tax accountants, they do. I never know what to say
to them except "Belt-up."

ANNIE: So why don't you listen? You might learn something.

PADDY (*depressed*): I'm not interested in things that don't interest me.

ANNIE: Paddy, what are you afraid of?

PADDY: Me? I'm afraid of being stupid.

ANNIE: You want to do something about it?

PADDY: It's not that simple. I'm afraid of being stupid all right, but I'm more afraid of not being stupid. You know what I mean? Maybe stupid's not the right word. Naive. Innocent. Direct… (*Ironically*.)… Talented. No, it's probably stupid. But I'm afraid of stuffing my head with a lot of phoney nonsense. I'm afraid of getting all arty and pretentious and complicated and making easy things hard for myself. I let my instinct carry me through my roles and so far it works—even though I do have to look up a lot of words in the dictionary, I trust it. That and something else. You know these flowers I bought you tonight? I was ready to take a swing at you for making fun of me about them, but the next minute everyone was laughing and I forgot about it. You know why? Because they were laughing at me. As a kid, once one of those travelling fairs came to town, and I went by a booth and watched them shying coconuts at a clown's head. Well, that kept sticking with me though I couldn't figure out why, until my first big audition. There I was all alone on a stage and a proper clown I must have looked too. Somebody giggled, I remember, and somebody groaned, "Oh no," as I walked on. But it didn't worry me, that's the point. All I could think about was that clown. They come at you with their coconuts and murder in their eyes and instead you make them laugh. There's a thrill in that. It's magic. I don't mind them laughing at me. I don't mind them trying to knock me down either. It doesn't hurt me. I'm made of wood like that clown's head. And when I've got them, I can make them laugh or cry or anything I please. As long as I'm a nice stupid block of wood.

ANNIE: You could get into trouble with all this empty vessel jazz.

PADDY: You take my agent. Real high-pressure American-type agent. Born in Leeds. You got to read, boy, my agent keeps saying to me. You got to read. I read, what makes you think I don't read? You don't think I played two seasons at Stratford without reading the plays first? I don't mean that, says my agent. I mean books. Fiction. Best-sellers. Haven't got time, I say. Why should I? Most of 'em aren't any good anyway. All right, says the agent, if you haven't got time to read the books read the book reviews. Frank Sinatra—get this—Frank Sinatra used to read, read, read all day long, and then he got busy and didn't have the time, so he'd leave a stack of books by his bedside, and he'd read the book jackets before he fell asleep, so then he'd know the story. And he could go to a dinner party and start talking about some books and he could make better conversation about it than the people who'd really read it, says my agent, because he didn't get bogged down with details, see? But more important— now we get to the bottom of it- was that Sinatra knew the characters in these books. So he knew if there was a good part for him, in case they made it a film. (*Rises in sudden rage.*) Well the hell with that. What kind of a phoney am I supposed to be, going around spouting book- jackets? Look, someone's got a part for me. Fine, of course I'll read the book first, what kind of an idiot am I supposed to be? (*Ends up in a rage out of all proportion to what he's saying.*) I can read, for Christ's sake! (*Takes a book and drops it disgustedly. He is shaking all over.*)

ANNIE (*rising and going over to* PADDY, *touching him sympathetically*): Paddy, Paddy, you're all right, you know. You're doing fine. Go on being you.

PADDY: If I'm doing fine, then why am I so upset about my brother?

ANNIE: What's happened to him?

PADDY: Had a spot of news myself today. My kid brother's won a scholarship to Cambridge.

ANNIE: That's wonderful.

PADDY: Of course it is. I should be happy for him, shouldn't I? So why am I so depressed? I don't know. I always had us figured out as a pretty stupid family. Well I thought that's one worry off me shoulders. I won't have to shine academically. I'll have a go at it some other way. Now I wonder if I wasn't just being a lazy blockhead. It's a miracle I got off my bum long enough to trot round to acting school. Oh Annie, don't you see how much I need you? It's as if you were my bridge to the rest of the world. The way you go round digging into everything, questioning everything and sometimes in your questions I find my answers. I grow little green buds whenever I'm around you, little shoots of curiosity. They'd wither and die without you to water them. Stay here and get married to me, darling.

(*Knock on door.*)

ANNIE: Yes?

DOORMAN: All right to lock up now, ma'am?

ANNIE: Come in. You're new here, aren't you?

DOORMAN: Yes, ma'am.

ANNIE: Do you know my name?

DOORMAN: Just a minute. (*Consults list.*) Oh yes. Miss Fox, is it?

ANNIE: That was you on the switchboard this evening when I had a telephone call who said you couldn't find my name on the staff list, wasn't it?

DOORMAN: Yes, ma'am, I'm afraid it was. This is my first job ever, you see. I'm just the relief for Mr. Davis. He's down with 'flu.

ANNIE: I see. Well you don't lock up until you see me leave the building. Got it?

DOORMAN: Yes, ma'am. Sorry, ma'am. I'll try to get it all sorted out.

ANNIE: That's O.K.

(*He leaves.*)

(*To* PADDY.) Hey, how about that? That's fame.

PADDY: Annie—will you marry me?

ANNIE (*faintly*): Not so fast, boy, not so fast. Let me catch my breath. (*Puts on her coat.*)

PADDY: Where you going?

ANNIE (*baffled, points to the door then looks at him. Stops dead in her tracks*): I don't know. You've thrown me. I never thought of you as being possible.

PADDY: How do you mean, possible?

ANNIE: I mean as opposed to impossible. I've always gone for impossible men. Deliberately. The three big loves of my life, up till now, were a drummer who was married, a director who had been married five times thank you and good night, and a very well-known French singer who had three words of English to my five of French. And what I liked about them—what I went for—was that I could learn something from each—I even learned to play the drums—but at the same time I always had this built-in escape clause so that when the big question came up—go or stay—it never really came up. And when I started going with you and we started living in our dressing-rooms and going on the town, I thought goody what a lark, he's impossible. But now if you're going to be possible, I'll have to think it out all over again. Not that I don't love you—I really do, I love you more than I loved all three rolled up together, but I've got this thing against marriage, you know. I feel if I do any of the things, I mean one single one of the things my mother did, I'll turn into her.

PADDY: Am I anything like your father then?

ANNIE: God no.

PADDY: Then why should our marriage be anything like your mother's?

ANNIE: You're really serious about this?

PADDY: Aye.

ANNIE: You think we can make it?

PADDY: I know we can.

ANNIE: Then yes! Why not? The hell with New York. I'll call my agent first thing tomorrow. (*Kiss.*) A big yes. So where'll we end up tonight?

PADDY: I've still got the key to Gil Fletcher's place. He's not coming down from Stratford this week-end.

(ANNIE *goes to take a last look at herself in dressing-room mirror, he goes over.* ANNIE *grins delightedly.*)

(*Talking to her through the mirror*): We look good together. That what you're thinking?

ANNIE: No. More. I was thinking about what that Labour M.P. said. We stand for something. Kilmartin, what do you stand for.

PADDY: I don't know. The Potato Famine, I suppose. (Stops and picks up flowers.) What'll we do about the posies? Daft of me to get them for you on a Saturday night. Shall we take them with us?

ANNIE: No. (*Places them back in vase and puts them dead centre of dressing-table. They are in full bloom.*) We'll leave them at the altar.

(Exit together.)

Next scene follows on after they have left. It has begun to rain.

SCENE III

N.B.: Lighting and sound effects in this scene should be done as delicately as the storm in the Moscow Arts production of Uncle Vanya. *Light changes from light-dull to ominous-dull, down to threatening, into loud rain mixing with sound and wind. A gust of wind through half-open windows blows the sheaf of telegrams that* SARAH *picked up down on to oar.* DOORMAN *enters. Stands in middle of dressing-room wondering what to do. Another gust of wind and rain, etc., makes him realize the rain is coming through the window.*

Sees telegrams on the floor. Slow-wittedly picks them up, stands wondering what to do with them, finally pieces together where they belong and, standing on divan, puts them back up again. Stands in centre again. Gusts of wind and rain, etc., finally penetrate to him that window is open and rain is coming through. Goes over and closes window. This makes telegrams fall down again. DOORMAN *notices this. Goes and picks them up and stands with them in his hand again, wondering whether he should put them up or not. This is a weighty decision. Decides not to. Another thought is forming in his mind. It clicks. Deliberately and furtively he crushes telegrams into a ball. Looks round for place to put it in to conduct his experiment. Decides on waste-paper basket, puts ball of telegrams in basket and sets fire to it. Then turns and gets fire extinguisher and puts out the fire. It actually works. A look of beatific satisfaction crosses his face. The curtain falls.*

END OF ACT ONE

ACT II

SCENE I

ANNIE—HENRY RATTNER.
Place: Dressing-Room.
Time: Around 6:00 p.m.

ANNIE (*entering first, suede coat, black stockings, with milk bottle under arm, followed by* HENRY RATTNER): Come in, Mr. Rattner,   I come in. You been hanging around out there long? How awful!

HENRY: Only a few minutes, really.

ANNIE: No, but when I saw I was running late at the hairdresser's I telephoned them to let you into my dressing-room. What happened?

HENRY: Don't know. I have the impression the man at the door's not awfully competent.

ANNIE: He's the understudy, or replacement, or whatever you call it, for the regular doorman who's down with 'flu. God help us until he comes back. This lunatic left my milk standing outside the stage door all day in the rain. How do you like that?

(ANNIE *puts milk down, takes off her coat, scarf, etc., and during this registers that something is wrong with the room. Locates it as missing sheaf of telegrams from screen. Searches round divan, under pillows, behind divan and finally under it.*) Now what do you suppose he's done with those telegrams? Probably burned them! (*Back to* HENRY.) Sorry I couldn't speak to you at the hairdresser's. I was under the dryer. How'd you know I was there anyway?

HENRY: I rang your mother. She told me.

ANNIE: Of course. Good old Moma. Likes to keep tabs on her little baby. When she can.

HENRY: But why aren't we meeting at your flat? Or do you always get to your dressing-room this early?

ANNIE: Man, this *is* my flat. I live here.

HENRY: You live here? What do you mean? You've got no place of your own?

ANNIE (*pointing to various things*): Bed. (*Points to cupboard.*) Clothes, telephone, drinks. (*Picks up milk bottle.*) Kitchen. (*Points to shelf of books.*) Library, piano—they left it in my dressing-room because they didn't know where else to put it. Oh, and bathroom down the hall. What more could I want?

HENRY: But this is sheer escapism.

ANNIE: You bet it is. With rents what they are, think of the money I escape paying. The only snag is, I have to leave here some time at night and they don't open up until ten in the morning.

HENRY: But where do you sleep, then?

ANNIE: Here and there. I've got plenty of friends and they've got plenty of room. Well, they've always got an extra bed or couch is what I mean.

HENRY: But the lack of security, the lack of stability inherent in this mode of existence. It's monstrous.

ANNIE: An artist should be as free as a bird, no?

HENRY: Surely you're exaggerating this particular aspect of freedom out of all proportion.

ANNIE: Ah well…it's going to stop pretty soon, I guess.

HENRY: When you go to New York, you mean?

ANNIE: How'd you know they'd asked me to go to New York? Oh, Moma, of course.

HENRY: No, not your mother. That's what I was starting to tell you when I had my sneezing attack the other night. I'm Herb Greely's assistant.

ANNIE: Then you're putting on this show? Oh, no. This world is too small.

HENRY: A conclusion I believe I attempted to articulate at the time. Ha! Ha! (*He chuckles at his own wit.*)

ANNIE: Yeah…I believe you did.

HENRY (*suddenly serious, puckering his brows*): Actually I've been here for a couple of weeks already. I've been studying your performance to see if anyone in America could play it. Frankly, I think no.

ANNIE: Thanks. A bit sneaky and underhand, but let that go.

HENRY (*expansive gesture*): A half-million-dollar investment's at stake….

ANNIE: Sure, sure. I understand. I said let it go.

HENRY: No. I want to give you my frank and honest assessment of the situation. I would not be happy with myself for giving you anything less. As far as your presentation of the role goes you must recognize that—fine as it is—there is room for that intangible thing we call variety or taste, even from those who operate from the same basic principles and I'm sure you would be the first to say thank God for that—

ANNIE: Thank God for that—

HENRY: —so what I've had to ask myself during these two weeks as an observer is whether another presentation—another interpretation, if you will, of the role would be—not more valid: validity is, after all, relative—but would the values of the play be better served by the work of another actress? Personally I don't think so. Candidly, I believe that the qualities instinctual in you, which you are projecting into the part, exactly dovetail with this production, the significance of which cannot be grasped through exposure to anything less than the whole.

ANNIE: Thanks…or thanks I think. But after all that, I'm afraid I've already decided not to go.

HENRY (*leans forward*): Not to go? Why?

ANNIE: Well…oh, dear…. Personal reasons. I'm awfully sorry but I just can't tell you at present. Damn! that reminds me—I forgot to tell my agent too. It's the hairdresser; it always turns the day topsy-turvy.

HENRY: But you've got to tell me. Look here, we're entitled to know.

ANNIE: No you're not. What's Herbert S. Greely to me? Or me to Herbert S. Greely for that matter, besides a half-a-million-dollar investment? And what's half a million dollars between strangers?

HENRY: But can't you tell *me*? We're not strangers, are we, Ada? We go way back.

ANNIE: You know I don't want to break your heart or anything—but I can't remember you at all.

HENRY: You're not serious, of course.

ANNIE: Yes, I am. Why?

HENRY: Ada, I don't believe you.

ANNIE: It's true.

HENRY: Come on, try, Ada, try.

ANNIE: I am trying. It's all dark and shadowy though. I know you all lived down the road from us during the war…. Rene!

That's your sister's name. And then it gets all shadowy.

HENRY: Why?

ANNIE: Let's see. War.

> (*Poet and Peasant Overture.*)

Ta-tum, ta-tum, ta-tum-tum-tum. Ta-tum, ta-tum, ta-tum-tum- tum. We were evacuated. War over. We came back. Did you?

HENRY: For a couple of years. But I thought you'd remember me for sure because of the evacuation. In all sincerity can you ask me to believe you've forgotten that?

ANNIE (*annoyed*): Oh for God's sake, I give up. Tell me already. I swear I don't remember you.

HENRY: And yet we changed places once. Or rather I changed places with you.

ANNIE: Changed places with me? What're you talking about?

HENRY: It was during the evacuation. We were all to be evacuated on a certain date, remember, only you got scarlet fever and couldn't go. So your mother took me because she couldn't get out of London without a kid, and my mother took Rene.

ANNIE: I don't believe you. You're lying! What're you trying to say? My mother left me dying of scarlet fever and grabbed you to get out? Say that again and you're going to get your head handed to you.

HENRY: Look, it was no secret. I don't understand. You knew I'm sure. We all discussed the plan. You went to hospital and it was arranged that some woman was to bring you to the country five weeks later—or whenever it was you were out of quarantine.

ANNIE: No, you must be lying. Of course you are! I asked my mother what you looked like, the other day, and she couldn't remember.

HENRY: Come to think of it, what was there to remember? She took me to Wales and I was sent straight to school. I was away at school all during the war and mostly away at school when we moved back and then I emigrated to America first chance I got. You probably didn't see much of me after you were six.

ANNIE: No, that's not why I don't remember you. (*Sits down and stares at him, shaking her head. Slowly.*) Funny, I always thought of my mother being a bad mother—you know: bossy, possessive, prying and all that in the usual sense. But as far as her being a *bad* mother—or do I mean a bad *mother* in the real sense—that knocks me out.

HENRY: What do you mean, a bad mother? What did she do that was so bad?

ANNIE: Oh, come on—

HENRY: What could she do? You were in hospital, you couldn't be moved. Your father had his bad leg, she had to look after him.

(ANNIE *just looks at him steadily.*)

You're dramatizing the situation. I'm sorry to have upset you. I had no idea...well, I just had no idea.

ANNIE: Yeah...I'm sure if I confronted her with this that's just what she'd say: What did I do that was so bad, it was only a month and I had to look after your father and all that. But I remember what it was like for me. I remember having scarlet fever and being without my mother and it seemed that it was something I was being punished for and locked up in a dark room. And they kept my mother from me and I wasn't allowed to see her until I was good again. She said, "You be a good girl and I'll take you to the country." But she never came back for me. But you're right: the way we all lived on top of each other I must have known what was going on. So I didn't trust her. I never trusted her. I've been trying to trust her and knowing I can't trust her all my life. Mother. This is weird. Why does it hurt so?

HENRY: Merely because you're having trouble adjusting to the fact that she's a person. She's not a bad mother, she's only a person.

ANNIE (*pause—kindly*): Thanks. By the way, I still don't remember you. But I believe you were there, Henry.

HENRY: Well, then, for old time's sake tell me why you've decided not to go to New York.

ANNIE: I'm getting married. I think.

HENRY: What do you mean, you think?

ANNIE: I've only thought about it for a couple of days now. It's kind of new to me. Tell me about my father. Make him into a person for me.

HENRY: The only thing I remember about your father is that he always wanted a boy.

ANNIE (*depressed, bitter*): Yeah, I remember that too, come to think of it.

HENRY: Annie, make a clean break with the past. Come to America. That's what I did and believe me I don't regret it for a moment. You must be aware that the British Caste System is a self-perpetuating machine. Any objective exploration in what you may feel to be solely the psychological disorders in your background must take that into consideration as well as the obvious social and economic factors. You won't find real happiness until you've left all that behind.

ANNIE: The language barrier is beginning to fascinate me. I don't know what you're talking about.

HENRY: Very well, let's put it this way then: London is a one-horse town. I come back to it and frankly I'm amused. Oh, you've had more than your fair share of success over here, I'll grant you that. But you don't know what success is like until you've tasted it in New York. You can't imagine what it's like to have the whole town, literally the whole town, at your feet.

ANNIE: Oh, I can imagine it all right. And I'd love it. But that's the same town that turned its back on me a year-and-a-half ago, so I wonder how seriously I could take the adulation. Maybe you've got to be an American to really enjoy America. Mind you, I don't think it has anything to do with where you were born. I think Americans are being born all over the world now. I think you're an American. But I wonder if I am.

HENRY: Annie—try. See.

ANNIE (*taking a big breath*): Nope. Not this time. Marriage first.

(*Knock on door.*)

Yes?

SARAH: It's me, Annie.

ANNIE: Come in, darling.
> (SARAH *enters, rain apparel, carrying a big box.*)
> How'd you get through the iron curtain?

SARAH: I waited until he wasn't looking and then I sneaked through. (*Puts box down on divan.*)

HENRY: Well, I'll be leaving you now. But I'm going to keep on after you.

ANNIE: You're wasting your time, I'm afraid.

HENRY: Well, I've a week more. I'm staying at the Connaught

if you want me.

ANNIE: Good luck.

HENRY: Bye for now.
> (SARAH *has her back to them by now and is unpacking the box.* HENRY, *on way out, pauses by her side, suddenly bending over her closely, very come hither.*)
> Caught you on Teevee Sunday night. (*Makes gesture of an O with thumb and forefinger.*) Great!

SARAH (*jumps a little, startled*): You caught me *what*?

HENRY (*looks at her keenly and realizes mistake*): Oops, sorry. (*Chuckles humorously at his error.*) Wrong gal. (*To* ANNIE.) She looks exactly like whatshername, doesn't she?

ANNIE (*leading him out, deadpan*): Yeah…. A little.
     (HENRY *exits.* ANNIE *comes back to centre.*)
That was the Rattner boy.

SARAH: Yes, I know. What did he want?

ANNIE: He wanted to turn me into an American, I think. But just in passing he turned me into putty.

SARAH (*stops unpacking box for a moment*): What is, Annie? You do look odd.

ANNIE: My— No. I can't talk about it. It's too corny. Oof, it hurts. I thought I could talk about anything under the sun but I can't— Oh, what's the use. Hey, Sarah, what do you think of yourself as? Do you keep saying to yourself "I'm British"?

SARAH: You know I don't think of myself as anything.

ANNIE: No. I didn't think you did.

(ANNIE *laughs. During following scene, depression caused by the previous one keeps working on her and though she snaps out of it from time to time her temper is short.*)

SARAH (*going back to box*): I want you to try this on. I don't think I've got it quite right.

ANNIE (*for a moment diverted*): Oh goody! I can't wait.

(ANNIE *stands facing audience,* SARAH *helping her into the dress, covering her.* SARAH *steps back and reveals that new dress is exactly the same as the other one* ANNIE *was wearing.*)

SARAH (*anxiously*): How does it feel?

ANNIE (*moving experimentally, stretching, wiggling, etc. Goes and opens cupboard with full-length mirror and studies it. Very intent. This is to her a brand-new dress. Enthusiastically*): Wonderful, it's just wonderful. You've got the hips perfect.

SARAH: I set the panels in a quarter of an inch higher this time.

ANNIE: Brilliant.

SARAH (*critically, shaking her head*): Miles too long. See? (*Reaches down and rolls up hem with one hand an eighth of an inch. Drops to her knees. Takes pins out of a box and, putting them in her mouth, begins to pin up length.*)

ANNIE: Hey, I've just had a terrific idea. Next time let's do it in…white! Oyster white with maybe just a touch of blue. D'accord?

SARAH (*mouth full of pins*): Divine!

(ANNIE *suddenly spots wilted flowers. Dashes over to them. Kisses them and buries her face in them.*)

ANNIE: Oh, poor loves. You're all dead.
        (SARAH *follows over to* ANNIE *on her knees.*)
No, no, I won't throw them out. I'll press them. (*She sits down lost in a dream.*)
        (SARAH *waits patiently to get on with the dress.*)
(*Snapping out of it, stands up.*) Sarah, baby, how would you like to make me a wedding dress?

SARAH (*leaning back on her heels, spits out pins*): What? Oh no!

ANNIE: What do you mean "Oh no"?

SARAH (*goes on pinning*): I mean what for?

ANNIE: Oh, Sarah, I thought you were a bit brighter than that. To get married in, of course.

SARAH: Married? You?

ANNIE: Yes, married, me. What is this? Don't you believe me?

SARAH: Of course I don't! I mean it's against all your principles, isn't it? It's—it's like giving up, or giving in. Why only last week you told me the day you decided to get married would be the day you threw in the towel.

ANNIE (*carefully controlling her temper*): You don't think it advisable to get married then?

SARAH: Certainly not! What about New York for a start— What about—

ANNIE (*suddenly flaring up, stamping her foot*): Get out of my hair, will you? You're always underfoot. You're always hanging about in my hair underfoot. (*Defiantly flinging it out.*) You queer for me or something? (*Then more resolutely, deciding to make an issue of it, confronting her face to face.*) Face it, you're queer for me, aren't you?

SARAH (*back on heels. A pause, and then she roars with laughter, clapping hands together*): No, I'm not.

ANNIE (*pause*): You're not?
> (SARAH *shaking her head vigorously no.*)
> (*Disconcerted.*) You sure?

SARAH (*shaking head vigorously yes*): Positive!

ANNIE (*now really lost*): Oh. (*Pause.*) Well, what is it then? Why are you always around?

SARAH (*very simply*): I don't know what else to do with myself, and I like you so much—you're such fun, Annie, and I like all the people I meet with you. I know this sounds awful, but I like the people I meet through you.

ANNIE: Like who?

SARAH: Like all of them. Paddy for instance....

ANNIE (*sorry for her*): So you meet them, you poor schmuck, it isn't just meeting people. You're getting too old to be a walking fan club. It's no good unless you become involved with them. Mix it with them. Sleep with them.

SARAH: But I do.

ANNIE: What?

SARAH: But I do sleep with them.

ANNIE: Who?

SARAH: Well...you know...quite a few of them.

ANNIE (*unbelievingly*): Paddy?

SARAH: Yes.

ANNIE: You *what*? You slept with him? Get out. Get out, you slut!

SARAH (*up, backing away*): It still wasn't real, Annie. It all faded away the next day like it always does. It was just children's games. Anyway. I thought I was supposed to. I mean isn't it what you all do all the time—have a ball? Isn't it part of it?

ANNIE (*sits down, head in hands*): Oi-vey! Yes, it's part of it. You got me there, Sarah. I'm jealous though. Wait. What am I jealous about? I still like him and I still like you. But he—you—my mother—betrayed me. No, I've got to look at this separately or I'll go mad. How many times? Oh, no, no, strike that out. Let me get this right. I don't mean that. I mean I do want to know, but there must be some other way of asking it. (*Telephone rings.*) Damn! (*Goes to answer it.*) Hello, yes? Who? Oh—O.K., let him in, let him in. Look, just let anyone in. That's right. Anyone at all. Annie Fox is the name—that's me. Dressing-Room Two. Got it? Cool. (*Hangs up the phone.*) He's learned to use the telephone, Heaven help us. He's beginning to love his work.

(PADDY *bursts in.*)

PADDY: 'Ullo loove. (*Nods to* SARAH.) I've just spent a very interesting afternoon whilst you were laying about over at t'hairdresser's, my serpent of Old Nile…lying in your pavilion—cloth-of-gold of tissue—
O'er picturing that Venus where we see
The fancy outwork nature; on each side…pretty dimpled boys, like smiling Cupids
With divers-color'd fans, whose wind did seem
To glow the delicate cheeks which they did cool
And what they undid did. (*Very Laurence Olivier.*)
Anyway whilst you've been there, I've been at a building in Marylebone Road—
(*Pained expression on* ANNIE'S *face.*)

—what's the matter, chuck?—wait till you hear—at a building in Marylebone Road getting some very interesting information about—(*registers* SARAH *and becomes elaborately mysterious*) ahem-you-know-what-and—

ANNIE: Wait a sec. (*To* SARAH.) Get out, Sarah, will you? I want to talk to Fagin alone.

SARAH: About this dress...I mean...do you want me to keep working on it?

(ANNIE *stares at her in admiration. Decides to forgive her.*)

ANNIE: Sure, baby, sure, you keep working on it. What the hell. Fall by tomorrow around this time and pick it up. (*Pause.*) You know what...you're the real flip, aren't you? The rest of us are a bunch of village cut-ups compared to you.

SARAH: I may be a little late. I'm starting my flying lessons tomorrow.

ANNIE: Your flying lessons?

SARAH: Yes...I've been thinking about the moon lately. (*She exits.*)

PADDY: Wait till you hear this, m'darling. It's so easy you'll never believe it. I went to this building, see, it's the Marylebone Town Hall not five hundred yards from where we were staying over at Gil's. Now: to get married, all you have to do is fill in a form saying you want to get married, establish a residence in the area for seven days, wait three weeks more and that's it. And guess how much it costs? Oh, this is the lov-e-ly part. Guess. Go on.

ANNIE: Half a crown.

PADDY: You're not far off, clever girl. Seventeen shillings and thrupence! Seventeen-and-a-bit. What do you think of that?

ANNIE: It's a bargain.

PADDY: I wonder what the thrupence is for.

ANNIE: Don't brood about it.

PADDY (*this sentence very slowly, full of impact, this means a lot to him*): *I've got it all worked out.* Listen—how's this— we get married end of June when our contracts run out, quiet like, and before they can get their cameras out of their cases we nips into a plane for abroad. Where d'you want to go? I've never been anywhere before so it's all equal to me.

ANNIE: No.

PADDY: Here, here, what's up, loove?

ANNIE: I've just heard that you and Sarah have been making it. Charming.

PADDY (*uneasy*): Only once. It was nothing....

ANNIE: When?

PADDY: Well...as a matter of fact that night I didn't show up for dinner with those film blokes.

ANNIE: Oh, God.

PADDY: Aw, now. That's all behind us, isn't it?

ANNIE: No, it's all around us. Behind us, around us, and worst of all, in front of us. (*Breaks down.*)

PADDY: Annie, love. I know, I know. I've been pretty wild—especially this past month—but you know what it is? It's realizing how much I love you. Gave me a proper scare that did. So I ran off in all directions. But it wasn't no good. I tell you those girls—they don't mean a thing. They kill me, they do. They knock each other over to get to me and when they do they say something challenging like "I hear you're lousy in the sack." That's supposed to make me want to sleep with them, see, to prove that I'm not. My pride's at stake, my honour. So off I go with them and somewhere along the line it comes through my thick skull what it's all about. Paddy Kilmartin, the great lover, the great seducer—that's a lot of balls. I'm not having me way with them—it's the other way round. I tell you when the moment comes—you know what I mean ?—when that moment comes—I'm not with them. I'm off all by myself, I'm not with them. Oh, Annie girl, you're the only one who doesn't use me. You give.

ANNIE: I give but I'm a one-at-a-timer, and what I'm giving to you I'm taking away from someone else—I'm not giving it to everyone else. That's the way it is.

PADDY: That's the way I want it to be. When you sprung that surprise on me Saturday night about America, it stopped me dead in my tracks that did. I couldn't catch me breath.

ANNIE: I wish you hadn't said that. I suspect that.

PADDY: Why, in God's name?

ANNIE: Because I've a low, mean, nasty, suspicious, petty, unforgiving nature. Protect me, darling. Oh, Paddy, protect me from myself.

PADDY: I will. I will, you'll see!

ANNIE: You will—truly?

PADDY: Aye…aye….

ANNIE (*softly echoing*): Aye.

(*They remain in their positions staring at each other.* MRS. BASSETT *has* knocked and then entered. *They remain motionless, oblivious.*)

MRS. B (*after a long pause. Loudly*): Hello!

ANNIE (*in daze*): What?…

PADDY: Betty! How long have you been standing there?

MRS. B: Not quite long enough to topple over.

PADDY: Jesus, Mary and Joseph, did I have an appointment with you? It's gone clean out of my head.

MRS. B: No, you didn't, dear, it's all right, but thank goodness I've found you. I've been searching all over town.

PADDY (*to* ANNIE): You know each other—it's Mrs. Bassett.

MRS B: Of course we do. Hello, Miss Fox.

ANNIE (*coolly*): Do we?

PADDY: Betty Bassett, Annie. My agent.

ANNIE: Oh, my God, of course! I was wondering why your face was so familiar. Hello.

MRS. B: Well—

ANNIE: Well…?

PADDY: Well…?

(*Pause.*)

MRS. B (*to* ANNIE): Oh, what a lovely old dressing-table you've got! Aren't you lucky? Why are you pulling such an awful face, dear?

ANNIE: Because you said lovely *old*—

MRS. B: What should I have said? It is old.

ANNIE: But that isn't what's lovely about it.

MRS. B: I'm confused. What do you want me to say? Look at that *what* dressing-table?

ANNIE: Just look at that lovely dressing-table. And then everything else you feel about it. Bring in the fact that it's old if you like and how it all came to be. I don't mind a history lesson. I object to the implication that everything that's old is automatically lovely.

MRS. B: But when you've got an antique like that—

ANNIE: But you know it's true. Yes! Lovely old, lovely old. It's like one word over here. You go away for a while and come back and see if it doesn't jump out at you a mile. Try it the other way round and you'll get what I mean. Oh, look at that lovely *new* dressing-table. See. Doesn't work.

MRS. B: Well, there's a perfectly good reason for that. The way they make things nowadays. Sloppy, slovenly, mass-produced….

ANNIE: Yes…not like the lovely old British Railway carriages or some of those lovely old British roads. (*Goes and pours herself out some milk.*) Anyone for some lovely old wet milk?

MRS. B: Not me, thank you. Actually I'd like a lovely old word or two with Patrick. It's rather urgent.

PADDY: Fire away, angel. What's new on the book jackets?

MRS. B: That, Patrick, is exactly what I want to talk to you about.

PADDY (*arm around* ANNIE): Yes? Go on.

MRS. B (*she would like to talk to him alone*): Oh. Well. Excuse me, Miss Fox. Business. It's a sensational opportunity for you, Patrick. (*Shows him the book.*) They're making a film of this.

PADDY: Sorry I—

MRS. B: I know, I know. You haven't read the book jacket. I do wish you had. I'm afraid this is another instance in which you would have done well to take my advice, Patrick. Anyway (*hands him the book*) do read it as soon as possible and find out what it's about. Bertold is the one they want you to play. We'll have the script in a couple of days. Stanley Kubrick directing! He's the one, incidentally, who's been beating the drums for you. Did you even know he'd seen your show, when he was here in February? He's mad keen on you. The rest of the cast is Rod Steiger, Christopher Plummer, Jean Simmons, Eva Marie Saint…

ANNIE: And fifty thousand camels…

(PADDY *has reaction of slight displeasure at* ANNIE.)

MRS. B: And Christopher Fry is doing the script. The timing is perfect. They want you beginning July, which gives us a chance to catch our breath for a few weeks. Oh, they're shooting it in Israel. There's nothing arbitrary about it. That's where the story actually takes place.

PADDY (*whose arm has dropped from around* ANNIE): Sounds terrific. Go on.

MRS. B: That's all I know so far. Except they want our reaction as soon as possible. I've already told them that you'll be free. But I think we should wire immediately confirming our interest.

PADDY: You bet I'm interested. I'm interested as hell. I'd say yes just on the set-up. Fry, Eva Marie Saint, Kubrick. How can I go wrong?

ANNIE: Sounds like some crummy epic to me.

PADDY (*teasingly*): Stay out of this, Annie. Stop competing.

ANNIE: Talk about muck.

MRS. B: Oh dear, it's really useless to discuss this properly since neither of you has read the book.

ANNIE: Have you read it? Come on, I'll bet you haven't.

MRS. B: I've read about it, and I'm reading it tonight, Patrick, and I want you to do the same.

ANNIE: Look, you two go on talking. I'll be in the bathroom throwing up.

PADDY: Stop it, Annie, you're being most offensive.

ANNIE: I think you're being pretty offensive too.

PADDY: Oh you do, do you? And just why?

ANNIE: If you don't know I'm not going to tell you!

MRS. B: Children, children, stop quarrelling.

ANNIE: Oh, go to hell.
> (*Shocked silence.*)
>
> (*Sweetly.*) Sorry, I thought for a moment you were my mother. That's the way I always talk to my mother.

MRS. B (*getting ready to leave*): Well, Patrick, now that I've found you I'll be pushing along. Make sure you're in my office first thing tomorrow morning. We want to get moving on this. Good-bye, Miss Fox. Thanks for the use of your dressing-room.

ANNIE (*smiles sweetly, shows her out, then*): Thanks for nothing.

PADDY: Why were you so bloody rude?

ANNIE: We, we, we. D'you dig that cosy "we"? We want to get moving on this. We should wire our interest. Oh help!

PADDY: No, that isn't it. Ordinarily that would have made you laugh. What is it, Annie? What's got into you? You don't seem too happy over these new developments. Israel, baby, Israel. The home country. How's that for a honeymoon?

ANNIE: Except I won't be there. I'll be in New York.

PADDY (*curtly*): O.K., now what? Spit it out.

ANNIE: I didn't notice you consulting me about your next move.

PADDY: I thought that was it. Look, Annie, I shouldn't have to spell this out to you, but I'm a man and you're a woman—

ANNIE: Thanks for the news.

PADDY: —and it's natural for the man to make decisions that concern him for himself without consulting anyone. I'm not going through the whole thing again. I said I needed you and I wanted you, but if you want to be my wife you're going to have to go where I go and go along with what I decide.

ANNIE: And if not?

PADDY (*deep breath*): If not, not.

ANNIE: Boy, there's a change of tone.

PADDY: That's right. There's a change of tone then. So let's not hear any more about New York.

ANNIE: I'm afraid you're going to have to. What am I supposed to be doing in Israel all that time? Standing around in a slip ironing your shirts while you keen over the Sunday newspapers? Hell, no, if I'm going to have to do that I'd rather do something else.

PADDY: According to the experts it's a pretty masculine thing for a woman to want a career in the first place.

ANNIE: Then according to the experts you're in trouble, brother. They think it's a pretty feminine thing for a man to want to get dressed up in someone else's clothes and prance around the stage every night making an exhibition of himself.

PADDY: That's a lot of cobblers.

ANNIE: So's what you've been saying.

PADDY: Can't you imagine how I feel as a man?

ANNIE: No, I must be too feminine. I can't possibly imagine how you feel as a man…. Oh, Paddy, don't you see how silly all this women are such strange creatures, men are such something-or-other sounds?

PADDY: Let's get this straight. You want me to turn this down so you won't have to be ironing my shirts in Israel. Is that right?

ANNIE: No, of course not. There must be some way to figure this out. Maybe I could go to Israel for a month and then on to New York. Some compromise. I wish I could make you understand. If I don't work I'm a mess. It's all wrong of you to ask me to give it up.

PADDY: No, it's much simpler than that. You're getting even with me, that's all. Because of Sarah. Or because of New York, or God knows what. You're right about yourself, you know. You do have a low, mean, petty, unforgiving nature.

ANNIE: Shut up! Shut up! Shut up, shut up! You should talk. You of all people. You're the most selfish man I've ever come across. I'm supposed to give, give, give, give, so that you can take, take, take…oh nuts to that!

PADDY: *You* give? Don't make me laugh! You give like an elastic band-snap. When things aren't going exactly your way and you take it all back. What's the matter, you afraid in the excitement I might forget to marry you? I'll marry you. I said I would, didn't I? Or are you jealous of Eva Marie Saint already?

(ANNIE *throws glass of milk in his face.* PADDY, *almost as an automatic reaction, slaps her face. Silence. They stand there. They look at each other as complete and disinterested strangers now. This can be achieved technically by the two actors dropping their characterizations and projecting simply themselves until* PADDY *leaves.*)

PADDY: I guess I didn't have it all worked out.

(ANNIE *is silent. They stare at each other for a moment and then* PADDY *leaves. After he goes* ANNIE *works back into her char- acter as it were. Begins to feel the pain. Looks at her- self in the: mirror and sings plaintively and expressively to herself.*)

ANNIE: Love, oh, love, oh careless love,
    You fly right to my head like wine.
    You have wrecked the life of many a gal,
    And you nearly wrecked this life of mine.
    (*Knock on the door.* ANNIE *flies in panic, first to telephone as if to phone stage doorkeeper not to let anyone in. Re- alizes this is futile. Starts towards closet as if to hide. Finally, with an impatient" Oh hell," under her breath, she decides to face it.*)
    Come in! (*She thinks it is* Paddy.)
                (JOHN CROSSLEY *enters.*)
    (*Dazedly, not knowing whether she is relieved or disap- pointed*): Oh…hello. Hello.

JOHN: Hello yourself. I've just come to say good-bye.

ANNIE: You're going away?

JOHN: From these parts at any rate. Don't laugh, but I'm going on a lecture tour. Here's the itinerary. (*Hands her piece of paper with schedule on it.*) Only this time I'm speaking to everyone. When you campaign, you can't help it, you mostly find yourself speaking to the people that agree with you already. This time I'm going to get my ideas over to the widest possible cross-section or I'll know the reason why. But not as a politician. That would be fatal. I've done some journalism in my day so I can lecture as a journalist: The Press and the Formation of Public Opinion and The Press and Distortion of the News—exposé stuff, see? and then right in the middle of the lecture, bam! They're going to get a polemic against the Immigration Bill. I'm going to get through this time. Your play has inspired me to present my views as dramatically as possible. And just as important as what I'm saying to them is what they're going to be saying to me. I'm going to find out first hand what they really believe in and what they're prepared to do about it, instead of trying to figure it out from those damn polls and reports.... I say, I've come at an awkward moment, haven't I? (*He has noticed that while* ANNIE *has been listening to him intently at the same time she has been tearing his schedule to bits.*)

ANNIE: Not at all, why?

JOHN: What are you doing that for? (*He glances at her hands full of the scraps of paper of his schedule.*)

ANNIE: Oh, my God! I'm sorry, I'm sorry. This is terrible. What can I do? (*She tries to put scraps together like a jigsaw puzzle on the dressing-table.*)

JOHN: It's all right. I've got half a dozen copies.

ANNIE: It's a terrible habit of mine. When I get upset I always start tearing up paper…I…I…oh, damn.

JOHN: Go on. Let me listen. If it's not butting in, maybe I can help.

ANNIE: I'm beyond help. I just broke up with Paddy—he just left two minutes ago. But it was close. The closest I've ever got.

JOHN: Not just a lovers' quarrel?

ANNIE: No, I don't think so. (*Sings gaily.*)
Love is like a fawcet, it turns off and on,
Love is like a fawcet, it turns off and on,
Just when you think it's on, baby,
It has turned off and gone….

(ANNIE *breaks down. Sits curled up in a ball, hugging herself and rocking. She is near hysterics but trying to get a grip on herself.* JOHN *drifts over to her book-shelf to leave her be.*)

JOHN (*reading out the titles of the books as if to soothe her, take her mind off her pain*): *Under Milk Wood, Nightwood, Pocket Oxford Dictionary, Twilight in Italy. Some Faces in the Crowd, The Cocktail Party, A Slight Ache, Plays and Players, Anatomy of Love, Cheri and the Las.t of Cheri, Mexico City Blues, John, Duke of Bedford, Background to Chinese Art. Leftover Life to Kill*….

(*Smiles at* ANNIE, *touched by the books.* ANNIE *tries to smile back.*)

ANNIE: Yeah…a little of everything. A lot of nothing.

JOHN: You're a darling, Annie. You'll be fine. I know it. (*Tries to kiss her.*)

ANNIE: Oh, I'll be fine. Sure, sure, baby-sweetie darling, I'll be fine.... (ANNIE *suddenly begins trembling violently. Turns to dressing-table and tries to pick up various jars; they all fall out of her hands. In a tight, controlled voice*) it's no good. I'm going to pieces.

JOHN (*alarmed*): Shall I try to find Paddy for you?

ANNIE: It's no good. Everything's changed in the last hour. All of a sudden no one's who they're supposed to be. My mother's not my mother—she's a person. My best friend's not my best friend, she's someone who shacked up with my boy friend. And my boy friend's not my boy friend, he's an actor—and a louse. Suddenly they're all people, all going about their business and they don't give a damn for me, and I'm alone. I'm all alone. (*Tries to open a jar and it falls on the floor.*) I'm ging to pieces. Now listen carefully to me because I'm going to pieces. Go out that door and find the Stage Manager—got it?—the Stage Manager, and tell him to get hold of the Understudy and tell him to hurry. I'm not going on tonight.

JOHN: I can't leave you like this....

ANNIE: Yes, you can. I know what's best. Get the Stage Manager and do as I tell you and come back in an hour. I'll have pulled myself together by then. Only hurry. Get the Under-study. Understand? The Understudy.
(ANNIE *pushes* JOHN *out the door. Comes back to mid-dle of the stage. Thought strikes her.*)
Oh my God—doctor's certificate. (*Goes to her telephone*

book on telephone table.) Doctor, doctor. (*Leafing through.*) Who the hell's a doctor? (*Closes book as thought strikes her.*) Here we go. (*Picks up phone.*) Stepney 5675. Right.... Hello? Hello, Moma? Listen, who's that quack doctor you're always running to...you know, the one that keeps knocking on wood every time he tells me how well I'm looking. Blackman? That's it, Blackman. Well, run over to him right now and tell him to write me out a certificate saying I can't go on tonight...wait a minute, will you...can't go on tonight, I've got flu. Yes. Temperature of a hundred and five. And come over here with it. No, *you*, Moma...(*begins to cry as curtain starts to fall*) *you*. Come over, do you hear? I need *you*....

CURTAIN

END OF ACT TWO

ACT III

SCENE I

Upstage Right, MOTHER *at wash-basin, holding head of* UNDER-STUDY, *who is dressed in costume we have seen* ANNIE *wearing at beginning of Act One, Scene Two.*

ANNIE, *all dishevelled, make-up streaked, is still in same dress as in previous scene, with pins sticking in hem-line. She is pacing up and down. Occasionally breaks her pacing to study the other two and then resumes.*

ANNIE (*scratching leg*): Christ, these pins keep sticking into me!

(UNDERSTUDY *finally finishes throwing up, with a groan.* MOTHER *leads girl gently to chair, centre. Girl sinks weakly into it.*)

MOTHER (to ANNIE, without turning her head): Wet towel.
(ANNIE *stops pacing, snaps to quickly and goes to basin to wet a towel.* MOTHER *speaking to* UNDERSTUDY.)
Here, there. Poor little Understudy (*She looks cluckingly at* ANNIE, *shaking her head sympathetically.*)

(ANNIE *responds by giving* UNDERSTUDY *a glare and scratching viciously at her leg again*.)

There, dear. That's just what you needed, you know. Best thing you could have done. I always used to give Ada a teaspoon of salt to get her din-dins up whenever her tummy was upset, didn't I? (*As she takes wet towel from* ANNIE *and places it on* UNDERSTUDY'S *forehead. Back to* UNDERSTUDY.) Feeling better now?

UNDERSTUDY (*wanly*): I don't know. I feel awful.

MOTHER (*leading* UNDERSTUDY *to divan*): Now you just lie here awhile and rest. (*To* ANNIE.) Get me that eiderdown, will you?

(ANNIE goes to cupboard.)

Come on, up with the footsies.

(ANNIE *gives* MOTHER *eiderdown and* MOTHER *covers* UNDERSTUDY, *fussing with pillows, etc. To* UNDERSTUDY.)

Now here's what you're going to do. You're going to make your mind nice and blank. That's right. Blank and smooth right down through your tummy to your toes. Deep breath now. Now think of something nice. (*To* ANNIE.) Freshen it for me, will you, love?

(ANNIE *does as told*.)

(*To* UNDERSTUDY.) Think of the first time you were allowed to wear lipstick.

(UNDERSTUDY *gives a weak little laugh*.)

That's right. Now you just rest. Everything's going to be all right. Try to get a little rest.

(UNDERSTUDY *smiles up at* MOTHER *gratefully*. ANNIE *sits in dressing-table chair, hunched forward brooding and*

81

scratching her leg.)

CALL BOY (*bellowing*): Half-hour!

ANNIE (*bellowing back*): Ta, love!

(UNDERSTUDY *reacts violently to this. Leaps out of divan and heads for basin.* MOTHER *quickly follows, trying to hold towel, which has fallen off* UNDERSTUDY'S *forehead, in front of* UNDERSTUDY'S *mouth.* MOTHER *is not quite quick enough and some of the vomit gets on the front of* UNDERSTUDY'S *costume.* MOTHER *leads her to basin.*)

MOTHER: That's the girl. You just let it come up. Let it all come up.

UNDERSTUDY (*gasping*): Nothing more to come.

MOTHER (*to* ANNIE, *giving her soiled towel*): Another towel.

ANNIE (*reacting to soiled towel*): Oh, God.

UNDERSTUDY (*helped by* MOTHER *back to chair centre*): Miss Fox, I just can't do it. It's too short notice. It's not fair. (*Appealing to* MOTHER, *clinging to her arm.*) She's never been off before and then suddenly, at the last minute, they pull this on me. (*To* ANNIE.) Are you sure you can't go on, Miss Fox? You look all right to me. I mean you haven't broken your arm or anything. Are you sure you can't?

ANNIE (*losing her temper*): Of course I'm sure. Why the hell do you think I sent for you?

UNDERSTUDY (*grumbling*): Well, you've never done it before.

ANNIE (*incredulously*): Look, didn't you imagine you were ever

82

going to play the part?

UNDERSTUDY: Yes, but I never imagined it would be like this. I haven't had time to do my preparation or anything.

ANNIE: What did you think all those understudy rehearsals were for?

UNDERSTUDY: That's different. Besides, I'm rotten in the part. I hate myself in it.

ANNIE (*banging her forehead with her fists*): Oh, God!

MOTHER (*tuts reprovingly at* ANNIE. *To* UNDERSTUDY): Come on, dear. You lie back down a little.
(UNDERSTUDY *goes back on divan.* ANNIE *drops back on dressing-table chair. Bangs her hair brush on table impatiently.*)
(*Sternly.*) Behave yourself, Ada. Be a good girl.

ANNIE (*exploding*): Good girl! (*Throws brush down with a bang.*) Hell, Moma, what's the matter with you? I'm suffering too, can't you see that? (*Pause while* ANNIE *stares at* MOTHER.) O.K. Let's have it out. Let's have it out once and for all. First of all I'm not a good girl. That's just first of all. Tell me this: what do you say to people when they ask you where I live?

MOTHER: Why I tell them you're looking for a flat.

ANNIE: Oh you do, do you? That's interesting.

MOTHER: Why, dear? It's true, isn't it?

ANNIE: No, it is *not* true. I live in this dressing-room because I like to sleep around. Do you know what sleeping around means, Moma?

MOTHER (*busying herself with dress box that* SARAH *brought* ANNIE'S *dress in. Begins folding tissue paper*): No, Ada, I don't.

ANNIE (*pressing on*): What do you think I do with the men I go out with, huh? Come on. What do you think I do?

(*A pause while* MOTHER *goes on carefully folding up tissue paper. She speaks finally, looking steadily at* ANNIE, *tissue paper in hand.*)

MOTHER: I don't know, dear. What do the other girls do?

ANNIE: What the hell's that got to do with it?

MOTHER (*simply*): I'm sure you do what all your other friends do. (*She turns away and puts neatly folded tissue paper in one of the drawers.*)

ANNIE (*despairingly*): I can't even call to you from across my century, can I?

MOTHER: I never heard such talk, Ada. Why you're twenty-three.

ANNIE: Twenty-five, Morna.

MOTHER (*neatly unknotting and winding up string from box*): Well, when you think the way things have changed in twenty-five years I suppose it's no wonder people have too. (*Sits down in centre chair.*) The year you were born they didn't have any passenger aeroplanes even. I remember one of your father's cousins—a mechanic—flew all the way from Canada on an Empire Flying Boat they were testing.

Such excitement. We all followed his route. Montreal—Botwood, Newfoundland—Foynes, Ireland—Southampton. They couldn't even land on land then, you know. They had to land on water. And now all you see is jets. jets all over the place—

ANNIE (*interrupting*): Oh stop all that! Moma, listen to me. (*Goes over to* MOTHER'S *chair, kneels and puts head in* MOTHER'S *lap.*) Listen to me, please. What would you say if I told you I was madly in love with someone and he's walked out on me and I…just don't know what I'm doing?

MOTHER (*stroking* ANNIE'S *hair*): Who is it, dear?

ANNIE: He's an actor.

MOTHER: Well, never mind. As long as it's what you want I'm sure it'll be all right.

ANNIE: But it won't. It won't! Can't you hear me? I'm miserable. I'm desperate. I want to die.

MOTHER: For shame, Ada. A big girl like you? Pretty, successful. Why you've got everything.

ANNIE (*laughing helplessly*): I'm not pretty, Moma; you know that. My nose is terrible.

MOTHER (*firmly*): Yes, you are pretty, Ada. You always were. You were the prettiest girl on our road. I always told you that; you never believed me, but I always told you that.

ANNIE (*hugging her*): And you're the best mother in the world. I'm sorry I get so awful to you. I don't know what comes over me. Just irritable, I suppose.

MOTHER: Want to come home tonight?

ANNIE: Oh yes, Moma. I never wanted to leave you. (*Rises slowly and confronts her.*) Why did you leave me, Moma? Why did you do it?

MOTHER: Do what, dear?

ANNIE (*backing down, suddenly scared, cannot go through with it*): Nothing. Nothing. (*Crosses over to dressing-table chair.*) Oh, go away. Go away and leave me alone.

MOTHER (*very quiet, staring off into the past*): How you used to love your Moma! How you used to cover up my photograph by your bedside with all your blankets at night so my picture shouldn't catch cold.
(ANNIE, *who has been building a tower of jars on her dressing-table, freezes as she listens to this new evidence of her devotion to her mother.*)
(*Sighs.*) Well, they all grow up, what can you do?

ANNIE (*softly to herself*): Yeah…yeah…they do. (*Then to* MOTHER, *not unkindly.*) Thanks for reminding me.

(JOHN *enters and takes in scene:* MOTHER *fooling with string in centre chair.* UNDERSTUDY *propped up on divan clutching stomach and making agonized faces.* ANNIE *at dressing-table now making different-shaped buildings out of jars.*)

JOHN: What's going on, Annie? You all right?

ANNIE (*swinging around*): Oh, hello. I'm all right. (*Nods in* UNDERSTUDY'S *direction.*) My understudy's not. (*Staring at* UNDERSTUDY.)

JOHN: What's the matter with her?

ANNIE (*also staring at her*): She doesn't want to go on.

JOHN: Doesn't want to go on!

ANNIE: That's right. Oh. This is my mother, John. Moma, John Crossley.

MOTHER: Pleased to meet you. Are you the actor?

JOHN (*smiling*): No, I'm the Labour M.P.

MOTHER: Oh. That's nice.

(*Tannoy: "Five minutes, please." They all stare at* UN-DERSTUDY, *who has begun groaning.*)

UNDERSTUDY (*sitting up, clutching stomach*): Miss Fox, please. I've forgotten everything. I can't even remember my first line. I can't remember any of my moves. I'll just make a fool of myself. Look at your costume on me. (*Stands up.*) It doesn't fit me any more. It's too small. I can't breathe in it.

JOHN: Good God. Doesn't she have her own costume?

ANNIE: With this crummy management? Are you kidding?

UNDERSTUDY (*working herself up*): It's choking me at the waist. It's cutting off my breath supply. I think I'm going to faint. (*Begins to keel over.*)

ANNIE: Smelling salts, smelling salts.... I don't know where she keeps them. (*Runs to door.*) Mrs. Turner, come in now, will you, and find me the smelling salts.

(MOTHER *and* JOHN *are propping up* UNDERSTUDY *on either side, holding her head down, etc.* ANNIE *and* MRS. TURNER *go over to her.* MRS. TURNER *gets smelling salts from nearby table.* ANNIE *holds then under* UNDERSTUDY'S *nose until she begins coughing.*)

UNDERSTUDY (*frantic and spluttering to* ANNIE): I'm scared. Don't you see I'm scared? How can you be so cruel? Please don't make me go on. Please. I'll do anything but please don't make me go on.

ANNIE: O.K., O.K. (*Moving fast, she rips off her own dress. Props up* UNDERSTUDY *and she and* MRS. TURNER *begin to undress* UNDERSTUDY *and dress* ANNIE.)

JOHN: What are you doing?

ANNIE (*continues undressing* UNDERSTUDY): What do you think I'm doing? I'm going on. (*To* DRESSER.) Tell them to hold the curtain five minutes. (*Stops what she's doing and turns to* JOHN. *A second's pause.*) Well. That just about completes my day. And my understudy's not my understudy. (*With wonderment.*) I'm my own understudy! (*She puts on the* UNDERSTUDY'S *costume. Slight reaction as she sniffs the front of the dress.*)

UNDERSTUDY (*helpfully*): I wiped it off where I got sick on it.

ANNIE: Thanks a lot. (*Gets huge bottle of cologne and splashes it all over front of dress.*) Oi! Oo, oi, oi! (*Sits down to dressing-table and very quickly and efficiently, with utter and complete concentration, makes up. Base. Eyes. Hair. With care. The rest of the people stand around well out of the way.*)

UNDERSTUDY (*snivelling and shivering in underwear*): You're an angel, Miss Fox. I'll never forget you for this, truly I won't. Please don't tell the stage manager about this, will you? I mean it would finish me.

ANNIE (*going on with combing her hair*): Sure, baby, sure. Just pipe down for a minute like a good girl, will you? (*To* JOHN.) I see why we go on. Living, I mean. It's no mystery. He (*pointing heavenwards*) won't let you not!

MOTHER: That's right. You're a good girl, Ada.

JOHN: Shall I go?

ANNIE: Yeah. Come back later if you can.

JOHN: I'm supposed to be catching the 11:40 to Leeds. I lecture there tomorrow morning. But I can cancel it. (*He puts his head on hers and looks into her eyes. This is in fact a proposition. A pause.* ANNIE *considers.*)

ANNIE: No. No. Go ahead. Don't stop the flow. There's always the next thing to do, isn't there? That's the way it's laid out. Oh, that reminds me—by God, it does! There is something you can do for me. Call my agent. No. Call the Connaught and ask for Henry Rattner. Tell him I've changed my mind about coming to New York. No, wait. Call him and tell him I'll call him in an hour. No, tell him— No, just tell him I rang. (*Pause.*) Boy I'm going to be great tonight.

(*Over Tannoy: Act One beginners please. Act One beginners please.*)

ANNIE (*to everyone in the room*): Better clear out and leave me alone for a second, huh?

(*They exit.*)

(ANNIE *alone. Goes stage centre facing audience. Long pause.*
She looks heavenwards and speaks as if addressing God.)

(*To God.*) Hey you up there—so who else have you been seeing
lately? (*Turns round and begins to exit on to stage.*)

CURTAIN

SCENE II

Dressing-room. Suit-cases open, but packed on floor. Room dis-
mantled of books, posters, telegrams, etc.

Time: After the show Saturday night a week later.

WILLY, SARAH, GRIFFITH, JOHN. *They are sprawled round dress-*
ing- room in attitudes of waiting.

GRIFFITH: The curtain's been down ten minutes. What's keeping
her, anyway ? Where the hell is she?

SARAH (*to* WILLY): What were you saying to me before about
Mrs. Turner?

WILLY: Oh, yes. Just as I was coming in here this evening I stum-
bled over Mrs. Turner out in the passageway carting off
some suit-cases.

GRIFFITH: So where was she going with them?

WILLY: Haven't a clue. As I assumed the suit-cases to be hers I didn't think to ask. (*Lifts some of* ANNIE'S *things from a suit-case.*) Apparently not. You know, I just have the feeling that Paddy's been giving our Annie a bit of trouble. Or— you don't suppose she's gone and done something disastrous, like eloping with him? No. She'd never without letting us know.

JOHN: Well, doesn't anyone know what's been going on? I only got off the train from Manchester about half an hour ago and came straight here.

SARAH: Don't look at me. Haven't seen Annie all week. Had to cancel my fitting with her because I've been too busy with my flying lessons. God, it's wonderful up there. You know, it feels like coming home at last. I—well, this is it. No more apologies for not being able to connect with Earth. It's Mars for me from now on.

WILLY: I think you're right, you know. I think you've been a creature from outer space all this time heavily disguised as a woman.

SARAH: So now I can drop the disguise. What a relief! What do you suppose has happened to her?

(Telephone rings. They all look at it. Rings again.)

WILLY: Ah! This may be our answer. (*Picks up phone.*) Hello, yes? Put it through. Oh. No, she's not here at the moment. Yes, yes, I've got it. She's to telephone you at Grosvenor 7070 the minute she comes in. Extremely urgent. All right. Good-bye.
     (*They all look at him expectantly.*)
That was the Rattner boy.

SARAH: Oh God, I hope it's not *him*.

WILLY: Well it certainly looks as though she plans to make her getaway.

JOHN: Or maybe she's already made it. What a crew! (*Looks at* WILLY'S *bandaged head and* GRIFFITH'S *bandaged finger.*) I'd say time has not dealt too kindly with any of us.

WILLY: What on earth's happened to your voice?

JOHN: Lost it talking too much. Shouting, in fact. During the campaign one was warned against getting into anything that looked like an argument. I've been making up for lost time.

WILLY: So what have you been shouting about?

JOHN: What I've been seeing. England is seething with frustration. little water-tight compartments of indignation erupting all over. And the trouble is nobody can bloody understand that their particular protest is directly related to the government. It's what I've been trying to tell this group of architects in Bristol who've been marching with placards protesting against the ugliness of a new set of buildings there. But no—to them architecture is architecture and politics is politics and the Government is something that sits in London on its bottom and spends all its time debating old issues it's never settled and never will.

WILLY: Well, isn't it? That's what I think of it as.

JOHN: That's what it will be until people learn to channel their protests specifically to where it counts and not just to the world in general.

WILLY: I don't know. I rather like the idea of sitting down outside something you don't like as a protest. Only I'm so lazy I'd prefer lying down.

GRIFFITH: I'm going to lie down outside Annie if she doesn't come back soon.

WILLY: Well I don't know what she's been up to. Actually I've been rather involved myself this week. A casual friendship quite unexpectedly flowered into a beautiful romance.

GRIFFITH (*pointing to* WILLY'S *bandaged head*): And that's the result?

WILLY: This, believe it or not, was the result of an accident. As I was leaning out of the window to greet my new-found friend, the sash broke and the blasted thing fell on top of me. Very nasty crack it gave me too. Well…it's the first time I can remember doing myself a mischief without meaning to. No, I hope it's not Paddy. I hope she hasn't decided to make some really big mistake like marrying him. I never breathed a word to her, of course, but I was always rather against that liaison. It's not her at all. Most un-Annie.

GRIFFITH: Yeah? What is Annie?

WILLY: Why, she's divine. I mean she's a great camp.

GRIFFITH: You mean you want to keep her in your camp. Look, I happen to know how much time she wastes bandaging your slit wrists and snatching away your sleeping tablets and generally propping you up over your silly carry-ons.

WILLY: I don't for a moment expect you to understand this, but I love Annie almost more than anyone in the world. And I want the best for her. Paddy's an insensitive oaf. He's not fit to be her chauffeur.

GRIFFITH: Ah, yes…all the old images….

WILLY: I apologize for being out of fashion. Is that what you want for her? Paddy? Be honest.

GRIFFITH: No, I don't. But not for your selfish reasons. She's a whole person as she is. A whole, beautiful, complete person. She gets hooked up with someone—anyone—and she's bound to be less.

SARAH: And she's got this chance to do the show in New York, you know. That's come through. She ought to stay free and unfettered. I think that's why I'm against it.

JOHN: Well, I know why I am and its much simpl—

(*Enter* ANNIE.)

ANNIE: What—oh—hello. Well. You're all here.

WILLY: All here and waiting. Would you very much mind explaining where the hell you've been, young lady, and what's the meaning of all this? (*Indicating suit-cases.*)

ANNIE: I'm doing a flit tonight. My agent found me a ser-veece flat-let in Mayfair. I can't afford it, but he's letting me borrow on my New York salary.

WILLY: And where have you been all this time?

ANNIE: Having a drink with some of the kids upstairs. I'm tired of this dressing-room. And everything in it.

WILLY: What a charming way to greet your guests!

ANNIE (*shrugs*): Sorry. (*Slumps on dressing-table chair.*) Help yourself. (*Indicates drinks.*) Mrs. Turner should be back soon for the rest of the stuff.

WILLY: Oh. Telephone message. (*Hands her slip of paper.*)

ANNIE (*grabbing it*): Yeah? Whyn't you tell me?

WILLY: It was the Rattner boy. He says it's urgent.

ANNIE (*slumping again, obviously disappointed*): It's always urgent. If he changes his socks it's urgent. (*Very low, head in hands.*) Who's got an overdose of seconal on them?

WILLY: Corne, come, Annie. Snap out of it. Remember that talking-to you gave me last month? I do. "I *refuse* to suffer," you said. "Oh, maybe I'm doing it all the time but I refuse to do it consciously. I won't just sit there and let it wash all over me...."

ANNIE: Yeah? That was the first lie.

GRIFFITH: What game is this?

ANNIE: It's called conversation. (*Low again.*) Only I don't think I want to play.

GRIFFITH: Pull yourself together, chum. All this moping around makes you very bad company. An energetic Annie is what we want, full of spunk and sparkle—not some old wet dishcloth. What's the matter?

ANNIE: Would you like to hear a résumé of my past week?

GRIFFITH: Sure—let's have it.

ANNIE: Monday—murder. Just plain murder. Tuesday—Matinee. Wednesday I went to three movies. Two during the day and the late show at the Academy. Thursday I went out looking. Friday I stayed in hiding. Saturday—Matinee.

GRIFFITH: So? it's Saturday night now. So cheer up, schmuck. Why depress everyone else?

WILLY: Yes, darling. This is most unlike you.

ANNIE: But look—I've got troubles. Yeah…come to think of it, Monday night, when all hell was breaking loose, not one person took a moment off to say "poor Annie."

GRIFFITH: Because you're not "poor Annie."

ANNIE (*incredulously*): I'm not poor Annie? (*She looks round incredulously. They all laugh.*)

SARAH: Certainly not!

ANNIE: Why can't I be poor Annie?

GRIFFITH: Because you're…you're… (*Gesture to indicate it's too obvious to put into words.*) …You know.

ANNIE: Because I'm young, pretty, successful? Because I've got everything?

GRIFFITH: Something like that.

ANNIE (*pauses and considers this carefully*): Can I never be poor Annie?

WILLY: Yes. When you're forty-five and slipping.

ANNIE: I see. (*Thinks this over. Looks at them all again and then back at* GRIFFITH. *Finally accepts this fact humbly. Lifts herself out of dressing-table chair and turns pointedly around so that she is facing into circle of her friends. To* GRIFFITH *in old hectoring tones.*) Nu, so what's new? What's that finger of yours doing all strapped up?

GRIFFITH: Banged it getting my new set up. Very painful indeed.

ANNIE: Good. I'm glad. I'd like to condemn you to spend an Open-Night on one of your sets. Just once. You'd hide under your bloody revolve—which by the way we had to get off and push tonight—it got stuck again.

GRIFFITH: We've heard all this before, Annie. Face it, I stole the notices.

SARAH: Oh, Annie, I must tell you. I'm completely caught up in this flying bug. You're going to have to find another couturier.

ANNIE: Honey-baby-sweetie darling, it's too much! You know I can't bear shopping. Wait! I've got it! It's beautiful! Listen to this: I've finally found a way to harness Moma. My mother—get this—my mother has never forgotten a shop window or a fashion photograph in her life. So, I'll send her into the field and she'll give me the low-down on the contents of every dress shop and dress show in London. And what's so groovy is that her taste is infallible. All she had to do is like something and right away I know it's wrong for me. How can I lose?

GRIFFITH: So are you happy now, schmuck?

ANNIE: Yeah, I'm beside myself with joy. (*Gets up and does little jumping step, snapping her fingers.*) Beside myself beside myself, beside myself with joy. (*Jumping "beside" herself at same time.*)

GRIFFITH: So what else is wrong? (*As if nothing could be.*)

ANNIE: Nothing. Well, I'd better phone the Rattner boy and see how he's getting on with his socks. (*Picks up phone.*) Let me have Grosvenor 7070. Mr. Henry Rattner—

(HENRY RATTNER *enters.*)

HENRY: Annie, here I am, save the phone call. Listen, something awful's happened. I've been trying to get hold of you all day.

ANNIE: Sorry, I've been avoiding this hole as much as possible. What is it?

HENRY: American Equity's turned down our request for you. Flat.

ANNIE: What? Why?

HENRY: You know their kind of reasoning. It's the part of an Italian girl so why do you need an English girl when you can get an American? I've been afraid of this all along—remember I told you—

ANNIE: Why didn't they check before they offered it to me?

HENRY: That's the whole thing. You have to be offered before Equity can turn you down. Look, I've got a car waiting outside to take me to the Airport. Gotta get back, they'll be casting first thing Monday morning.

ANNIE: Well—bon voyage.

HENRY: Yeah, we'll let you know.

ANNIE: Know what?

HENRY: We'll let you know who gets the part. (*He exits.*)

GRIFFITH (*very simply, not moving*): Poor Annie.

ANNIE (*stunned but very sweetly*): No. Don't go back on it now. Pour me a drink, will somebody?

GRIFFITH (*quickly*): Here, let me.

WILLY (*handing her a full glass*): I've already got it.

ANNIE (*swallowing large gulp, suddenly very brisk but with effort*): Won't be a minute, kids.

WILLY: We'll have a slap-up meal and get roaring drunk.

(*There is a strained silence on top of which* PADDY *comes in. A silence.*)

PADDY: Oh…. Where is she?

WILLY (*trying to get him out*): She's gone. Went away for the week-end.

PADDY (*going out of the door with* WILLY, *suddenly turns*): Here, wait a moment. What's up?

WILLY: Nothing's up. She left, I tell you. Just a few minutes ago. We're just about to leave ourselves.

PADDY (*louder*): What is this? The doorman told me she was

still down here.

ANNIE (*from behind screen*): Who is it?

PADDY: It's me.

ANNIE (*poking head out*): Oh… (*very taken aback*) it's you.

PADDY: Yeah. It's me.

ANNIE (*shaken*): Well, hello.

PADDY: Hello.

(*Pause.*)

GRIFFITH: Look, we'll be moving on.

ANNIE: No. No, stay.

PADDY: No, stay.

ANNIE (*to* PADDY): Have a drink?

PADDY: Thanks, I will.

(*No one moves.*)

GRIFFITH: It's late. Why don't we go and hold the table for you?

SARAH: Good idea. (*Pushing* WILLY *out.*)

ANNIE (*snapping out of trance*): Hey, what are you all leaving for?

JOHN: Shall I stay?

ANNIE (*holds on to him gratefully*): Yes. Yes, you stay.

(*They all file out murmuring "See you later". PADDY and JOHN stay. MRS. TURNER finishes tidying up.*)

(*Counting heads as they go.*) One, two, three, four, five, six. Ummm—I'll just telephone ahead and make sure of a table. Well, you know…one extra…. (*She is not really aware of what she is saying. Picks up phone.*) Hello? Get me Whitehall 4399. Hey…hey! Isn't that *you*, Mr. Davis? Well I'm damned. Listen—am I ever glad you've come back. How do you feel? Listen, don't move—never mind the number, I'm coming right up to say hello properly to you. (*Hangs up phone.*) Mr. Davis has just come back. (*Exits fast. They stare at her.*)

(*During next scene with PADDY and JOHN, MRS. TURNER sits down to dressing-room table, but, seeing a "stranger," i.e. John, pulls curtain round dressing-table as she makes up.*)

PADDY (*to JOHN*): How's everything?

JOHN: Fine. Just fine. Lost my voice.

PADDY: I see. I mean I hear.

JOHN: How're things with you?

PADDY: Fine.

JOHN: That's good.

PADDY: Yeah. It's good. It's great. (*Pause.*) How's the wife?

JOHN (*startled*): What? Oh, she's fine. Fine.

PADDY: And the kiddies?

JOHN: How did you know I had children?

PADDY: I didn't.

JOHN (*slowly*): I see.

(ANNIE *returns.*)

ANNIE (*babbling*): That Mr. Davis. He really is a darling! (*Shakes her head as if in wonder at it all.*) You know Mr. Davis, don't you, Paddy?

PADDY: What do you mean, I know Mr. Davis, don't I? I've seen him just about every day for the last six months, haven't I?

ANNIE: Oh—of course. How silly of me! I forgot; (*brightly*) you ought to meet him, John. You'd love him. You really would. He's been out all week. Had the—

PADDY: John has to leave, Annie.

ANNIE: What?

PADDY: John has to leave. He's got to get back home.

ANNIE (*still in a daze*): Oh?

PADDY (*clearly*): To his wife and kiddies.

ANNIE (this *registers on her finally. Looks at* JOHN *surprised. It is obvious it is the first time she has heard of his wife and children*): Oh.

PADDY (*cheerfully*): Bye-bye.

ANNIE: Oh. Uh—see you soon….

PADDY (*arm round* ANNIE, *pointedly*): Yeah, we'll be seeing you.

(JOHN *leaves.* ANNIE *and* PADDY *step apart, eyeing each other.*)

PADDY: You moving?

ANNIE: Found a flat. Just what was that all about?

PADDY: What was all what about?

ANNIE: The wife and kiddies. You could have knocked me over with a feather. How did it come up?

PADDY: As a matter of fact I brought it up.

ANNIE: *You* did ?

PADDY: That's right. I'm getting smarter by the minute. I takes one look at him and I says to meself, Paddy, me boy, I says, that fella's got a regular lecher's head on his face—

ANNIE: Face on his head—

PADDY: You know what I mean. Recognized it at once.

ANNIE: I'll bet you did. Well, well, well, well, well. (*Wickedly.*) And all this time I was afraid he was one of the possibles. Of course now that I know he's impossible that changes everything. En-tire-ly.

PADDY: You try any hanky-panky with that public servant and I'm going to stop paying me taxes.

ANNIE (*crossing. Over her shoulder*): I'll come and visit you with picnic hampers in jail.

PADDY (*plaintively*): I don't want to go to jail.

ANNIE: I know. You want to go to Israel.

PADDY: Ah! Now that's what I've come to talk to you about.

ANNIE: But that's what I wanted to talk to you about.

PADDY: Look, before you—

(MRS. TURNER *pulls back dressing-table curtain and emerges in bright red raincoat and black beret. They nod good night to her.*)

PADDY: Me first—

ANNIE: No—let me—

PADDY: Me first—

ANNIE: O.K. Go on.

PADDY: No, no. I'm sorry. You go.

ANNIE: No, you.

(*Pause.*)

PADDY: O.K. I just wanted to say I was wrong—

ANNIE: Oh, but that's just what I wanted to say I was—

PADDY (*a bit sharply*): Wait a minute, will you—that it would be daft of you to throw up everything just to tag on out to Israel with me. And it was mean and selfish of me to insist.

ANNIE: But I think you were right.

PADDY: Eh. How's that?

ANNIE: I think you were right to insist. You were right, Paddy. Right, right, right. And I was wrong.

PADDY (*annoyed*): I was wrong. God Almighty, can't you ever agree with me? I was wrong, I tell you.

ANNIE: You mean you don't want me to come to Israel with you?

PADDY: That's right.

ANNIE (*incredulous*): You mean to say you've come all the way over here for the sole purpose of telling me you don't want me with you? You're off your nut. Get out.

PADDY: No, it's not that. I came to tell you that I don't want you to come to Israel, that's right, but it isn't that I don't want you to come with me. I've thought it all over carefully and I've decided it's a bad thing for us just at this moment to put the whole world between us. I'd miss you too much—that's all. Not the way I love you. That's all. On the other hand I don't want to stop you going to New York. I know it would break your heart. So I just won't go to Israel. At least I'll be that much nearer to you.

ANNIE (*aghast*): You'd do this for me. Sacrifice yourself like this? I won't let you.

PADDY: Don't worry about me. Something will turn up. It always does.

ANNIE: Look. If you're going to give up Israel for me the very least I can do is give up New York for you.

PADDY: Oh, darling—if you would.

(*They kiss. They part. They stare at each other "in rapture" as*

*if in a play. Then uneasily they move away, each confused
and suspicious, not so much of the other as of himself.* ANNIE
*abstractedly studies her finger-nails. Sees a hang-nail. Bites
it. Wanders over to dressing-table mirror and looks at herself, more to examine her soul than her features.* PADDY *hov-
ers over her.)*

PADDY (*into mirror*): What is it?

ANNIE (*also in mirror*): I don't know. (*Pause, then blurts out.*)
   We don't look right. It doesn't feel right. What's wrong? Is
   it me?

PADDY (*uneasily*): Maybe it's me.

ANNIE (*decisively*): O.K. One more try. Please, please let me go
   to Israel with you.

(PADDY *loses his temper at this. Shakes her violently.*)

PADDY: I do not want to go to Israel one, twice, three times! Got
   that through your skull?

ANNIE (*dawn breaking at last, jumps up from chair*): Oh, you
   don't want to go!

PADDY (*striking his forehead*): Brilliant!

ANNIE: No, I just didn't get it straight before. Now I'm clear. So
   what happened to the part?

PADDY: Nothing happened to the part.

   (ANNIE *looks at him steadily and he becomes uncom-
   fortable. Stuffs hands in his pockets.*)

ANNIE (*again*): What happened to the part?

PADDY (*coming clean*): It was too small. (ANNIE *begins to giggle*. PADDY *fuming*.) That damned agent of mine. The book jacket forgot to mention that the character they wanted me for gets bumped off on page ten.

ANNIE (*laughing out loud*): Why you—why you two-faced baboon! Oh no, it's too funny— Hello, Willy, what're you back for?

WILLY: Thank God I caught you. We've walked out of the restaurant. For some extraordinary reason it's absolutely stuffed with everyone's ex-wives and ex-lovers and I don't know what. You never saw so many cross faces pointing out one's arrival. So we're having a nice cosy little supper chez moi instead. Drop round when you're ready.

ANNIE (*leading him out*): O.K., darling. Bye.

WILLY: Oh, and I suppose I owe you an apology, Paddy, for telling you Annie was out. After the bad news she had about American Equity turning her down I just didn't think she wanted to see anyone else. I shouldn't have taken it on myself. Am I forgiven?

PADDY (*pause while he takes it in*): Of course, of course. Think nothing of it.

WILLY: Oh, good. Well...later then.

PADDY: That's right.

(WILLY *leaves*.)

PADDY: So where were we?

ANNIE: I didn't know Willy tried to stop you seeing me. Funny how the people who are the most for you always seem to be the most against your having what you want.

PADDY: Never mind about Willy. He's all right. He means well. So where were we?

ANNIE (*in small voice*): You didn't want to go to Israel because the part wasn't big enough.

PADDY: And you didn't want to go to New York because—why didn't you want to go to New York, honey-baby-darling?

ANNIE: Because I wanted to be with you. Simple as that.

PADDY: Simple as that. Or simple as American Equity being stupid enough to turn you down for the part. That, *of course*, had nothing to do with your change of heart.

(*A long pause.*)

ANNIE: With my change of mind. There's been no change of heart.

PADDY: What's that supposed to mean?

ANNIE: It means my heart's always with my acting—that'll never change. Like yours. I gave my heart to it before I knew what I was doing and it's too late to take it back now. But my mind—my mind is on the main chance and if there was ever anything I've been sure of this past week it is that my main chance of happiness is with you.

PADDY: And you dared to call me a two-faced baboon.

ANNIE: But, darling—how was I to know you were going to find me out?

PADDY: Yeah…that's true. We're a right couple of first-class phonies, we are.

ANNIE: But at least—(*Breaks off, giggling.*)

PADDY: At least what?

ANNIE: At least neither of us got away with it.

PADDY (*smiles*): This time. (*Pause.*) I shouldn't be…but oh, Annie, I'm glad you're you!

ANNIE: And oh, Paddy, I'm glad you're you.

PADDY: So where does that leave us? Back at the beginning where we started?

ANNIE: No. I'm not interested in the beginning of a love affair. And I'm not interested in the end. Haven't you noticed they're all the same? It's only the middle that's ever different. Only the middle that's interesting. Let's go back to the middle.

PADDY: But if the same circumstances arise…

ANNIE: Baby, I'm afraid the same things are going to happen….

PADDY (*wanders over to the alarm clock*): I find—(*pause, as he tries very hard to put into words what he's feeling. Finally gives up*)—hmmm—I find life very complicated….

ANNIE (*sitting on divan*): Join the club.

PADDY: I mean it's—it's never what you expect.

ANNIE: That's what we voted.

PADDY (*his back to* ANNIE, *picks up alarm clock*): How late can we get to Willy's?

ANNIE: Twelve-thirty, I guess. Why?

PADDY (*smiling and turning around with alarm clock*): You'll be there.

SLOW CURTAIN

END OF PLAY

ABOUT THE AUTHOR

Elaine Dundy (1921–2008), born Elaine Rita Brimberg in New York City to Jewish immigrant parents, grew up on Park Avenue and was educated by a governess before attending Sweet Briar College, graduating with honors in 1943. A lively presence in New York's nightclub scene, she met figures such as Piet Mondrian before studying acting under Erwin Piscator alongside Rod Steiger and Tony Curtis. After working in Paris dubbing films, she settled in London, where she married theater critic Kenneth Tynan in 1951 and became part of the city's cultural elite. Dundy acted for radio and television before turning to writing. Her debut novel, *The Dud Avocado* (1958), became a bestseller, praised by Groucho Marx among many others. She later wrote *The Old Man and Me* (1964), *The Injured Party* (1974), biographies of Elvis Presley and Peter Finch, and a memoir, *Life Itself!* (2001). Dundy died in Los Angeles at age 86.

.

www.ingramcontent.com/pod-product-compliance
Lightning Source LLC
Chambersburg PA
CBHW020743130626
46554CB00006B/2121